To Live in a Gentle and Simple Way

To Love, To Learn, To Laugh, To Pray

David A. Enyart

Joseph,
This little book inspires and ministers to us. We hope that it will be a blessing to you, as well.
Love,
Papaw and Grandmother

Published by:
Tennessee Valley Publishing
PO Box 52527
Knoxville, Tennessee 37950-2527
Email: info@tvp1.com

Library of Congress Cataloging-in-Publication Data

Enyart, David A.
To live in a gentle and simple way / David Alan Enyart.
p. cm.
Includes bibliographical references.
ISBN 1-932604-07-3
1. Christian life. I. Title.
BV4501.3.E59 2004
248.4--dc22
2004009548

Printed in the United States of America

MAJOR AND MINOR CHARACTERS IN THIS BOOK

Major:

A COMPASSIONATE GOD who is able to do for us "immeasurably more than we think or imagine."

A CARING SAVIOR "by whose wounds we are healed."

A COMFORTING SPIRIT who "intercedes for us with groans that words cannot express."

Minor:

David Enyart: minister, professor, lover of God and family.

Mary Faith Enyart: beautiful wife, kind-hearted grandmother, gifted teacher, and devout believer.

Miss Adrian: Eleven year-old granddaughter. As a toddler, her favorite entertainment was to sit on pawpaw's lap and draw pictures.

Miss Allison: Nine year-old granddaughter. As a toddler, the self-proclaimed "boss of all the fairies."

Mr Kyle: Five year-old grandson. As a toddler he hit thousands of plastic golf balls with his plastic clubs, and slept at night with a real golf ball.

Miss Katy: Three year-old granddaughter. She always carries some soft, lovable, animal which she will gladly share.

Mr Andrew: Two year-old grandson. He was born with a smile on his face. All he needs to be happy is a tiny train and a bouncing ball.

Table of Contents

Introduction

Does your commitment to Christ make a difference in your inner world? This book is written for people who need God, though some may not realize how much they need him, nor the extent to which he is able to rescue them from the weariness of life, and give rest to their tired souls. By "rescue," I am not necessarily referring to miraculous deliverance from external circumstances, though I am thoroughly convinced that God does that on occasion. My central concern is the *heart and mind* of the believer. Chaos and anxiety often pervade our *outer world*. But how does a Christian rise above the turmoil and fear of our age, and find *an inner world of joy, peace, and contentment*? The Church Father Irenaeus once wrote: "The glory of God is a person fully alive . . . ." The purpose of this book is to assist believers in living life to the fullest. Jesus said, "I am come that they might have life, and that they might have it more abundantly" (John 10:10; KJV). The Apostle Paul asserted that believers could experience the *peace of God* which "transcends understanding" (Philip. 4:7; NIV). In the light of these Scriptures, I raise this supremely important question for people of faith: *Does your commitment to Christ make a difference in your inner world?* Is life difficult for you, *perhaps more difficult than it needs to be*?

Do you remember what Jesus said to believers who felt overwhelmed with the burdens of life?

> "Come to me, all you who are weary and burdened, and I will give you rest. [29] Take my yoke upon you and learn from me, for I am gentle and humble in heart, and you will find rest for your souls" (Matt. 11:28-29).

When we lose our perspective, when life gets to us, what should we do? The words of our Lord are simple, but, *when internalized*, they make a profound difference. Jesus said simply, "Come to me."

"Come To Me!"
(DAE)

"Heavy your load,
As you travel this earthly road?"

"Come to me!"

"A heart, dark and blue?"
"Yes, Lord, what must I do?"

"Come to me!"

"Anxious of tomorrow,
Filled with care and sorrow?"

"Come to me!"

"Lost your inner peace,
Searching for release?"

"Come to me!"

**"O my child, I know what's best;
Come to me, and I will give you rest!"**

I have discovered that to live the abundant life, *I must live in a gentle and simple way*. That means letting go of my worries and frustrations, and accepting *his rest*. It also means living at a slower pace—both on the inside and the outside. Most of all, for me, living the abundant life means allowing the Lord to be my constant Companion; I must habitually practice his presence. I think this is what the Apostle Paul meant when he wrote, “Pray without ceasing!” (Thess. 5:17; KJV). Several years ago, in a period of extreme stress and discouragement, I decided that I had to rethink the path and purpose of my life.

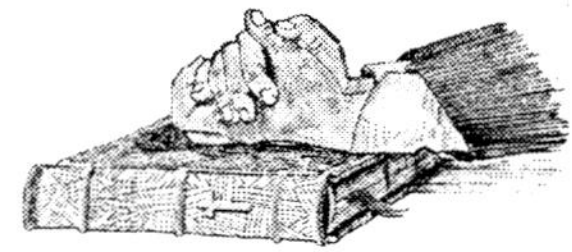

Though I declared myself a Christian, I was experiencing little of the “abundant life.” If Jesus came to give us “rest,” why was I so often tired? Things had to change; life in Christ could be better, and I knew it. I began, for the first time, a truly consistent devotional period for Scripture reading, prayer, and reflection. Little by little, with the Lord’s help, I began to quiet my inner storms—to *experience the abundant life*. I became more relaxed, less driven and compulsive. During that time, I wrote a life purpose statement which I continue to plant deeply in the soil of my heart. My supreme goal today and every day, until the Lord calls me home, is to live by that purpose statement:

Today!

To live in a gentle and simple way;

To love, to learn, to laugh, to pray;

To live in a gentle and simple way;

Today!

I want to live *one* God-honoring, Christ-exalting, Spirit-filled day at a time. *Each day* I want to love, to learn, to laugh, to pray. Granted, some days it's easier to follow that prescription than others. Regardless, each day I want to stay connected to my Heavenly Father, to practice his presence. And each day I want to stay in touch with myself, the self God has created and is creating. To maintain that dual connection with both God and self, I have a quiet time each day. This promotes intimacy with my closest Friend, the Anchor Point of my reality. During these periods of solitude and soul searching, I keep a spiritual journal for writing Scriptures, prayers, poems, devotional thoughts—anything that aids me in my quest *to know and love God more.* Also during my quiet time, I intercede before the Father on behalf of others. These prayers of intercession not only help the hurting, the lonely, the lost—they also assist me in becoming less self-focused.

Prayer: For Those Who Suffer

"Father, Help me to truly care for others. May I not be so absorbed in my own life, that I fail to feel for all who suffer. Teach me to make intercessory prayer a vital part of my everyday life. AMEN."

Prayer is the path to peace and patience; solitude and simplicity go hand in hand. Most often, life is good—if we have taught ourselves *to focus on the good*. And of course, life can be bad, if we have trained ourselves to focus on the bad. John Milton wrote, "The mind is its own place. And itself can make a heaven of hell, a hell of heaven." During a devotional time, I wrote the following verse which I entitled "A Fork in the Road."

Each day I come many times to a fork in the road;
Signs point in two directions.
This way, peace; this way, anger;
This way, joy; this way, sadness;
This way, gentle doing; this way, compulsive trying;
This way, relaxed acceptance; this way, irritation,
frustration, victim-hood.
Each moment of each day
I decide which fork to take; I decide!

The Apostle Paul said it so majestically, as reflected in Eugene Peterson's translation called *The Message*: "Summing it all up, friends, I'd say you'll do best by filling your minds and meditating on things true, noble, reputable, authentic, compelling, gracious—the best, not the worst; the beautiful, not the ugly; things to praise, not things to curse" (Philip. 4:8).

In learning to live a gentle and simple life, none of us dare say, "I have arrived!" We win this battle, or lose it, *one day at a time.* Though I remind myself daily of my purpose statement, I still have times when I lack the inner peace I need for a joyful, contented life. I still make some bad choices and must seek my Father's counsel and forgiveness. The habits of a lifetime do not easily surrender their strangle-hold on a human heart. But if we persistently *open ourselves* to our Father's presence and wisdom, *habits can be changed*.

In this devotional book, I invite you to join me *on a journey toward a gentle and simple life.* Travel with me on this golden path, as together we *love, learn, laugh, and pray.* Most of all, we will grow in loving and appreciating our Ever-Present Companion. The Apostle Paul declared: "Christ in you, the hope of glory" (Col. 1:27). Enraptured with that reality, I wrote this piece of verse, which I entitled "He Lives In You!"

He does not live afar on some distant star;

He lives in you!

He's not just "above" when you need love;

He lives in you!

You may feel forsaken—even by your own!
But in his love, you are never alone.

He lives in you!

So when life breaks you, and
no one will hear your story,

Remember: "*Christ in you, the hope of glory.*"

Let me say a special word about *laughter*: You will find this book sprinkled with chuckles. Sometimes I will call them “Humorous Interludes.” Along the way, I will also insert smaller units of humor which I shall entitle: ☺ “Smile Awhile.” Most of us take ourselves too seriously. When we genuinely laugh at something wholesome and good, life becomes a little more joyful and peaceful.

My prayer is that this volume will help believers live life to the fullest. That means, among other things, cultivating and enjoying *God’s presence*. The Psalmist accurately wrote: “Whom have I in heaven but you? And earth has nothing I desire besides you” (Psalm 73:25). May I say it like this: *If you truly have the Lord in your life, he is enough. If you don’t have the Lord in your life, nothing will ever be enough.*

Prayer: For a New Book

"Father, I am working on a new book. I shall call it, 'To Live in a Gentle and Simple Way.' I feel so excited about it, but also cautious. I'm excited because I want others to experience your love, your nearness, and your faithfulness. Yet, I'm cautious, because I do not want to present myself as some super-saint who lives ever on a spiritual mountain-top. I have ups and downs, hills and valleys; I shall be honest with my readers. You, Lord, are there for me through all my good times and bad times; I want to convey the joy of your presence to others. My God, I would that you and your Blessed Son receive the glory from this book. Father, thank you for loving us so. Teach us, as your children, to live the abundant life. May we, like Jesus, be gentle and humble of heart, and find rest for our souls. AMEN."

Chapter One

The "Inner World" and the "Outer World"

In the Eye of the Storm

(DAE)

"Lord, the storm rages, and I am afraid. Can you not stop the winds before they tear me asunder?"

"Child of mine, I hear your voice; I sense your fear. Someday I will tell the storm to cease its blowing. But, for now, it must rage on."

"But, Father, how shall any of us survive? We are frail, and the winds are strong!"

"My child, seek the eye of the storm, and wait for me; I shall come and calm your fearful heart."

"Yes, my God, yes! The storm still rages, but I sense your presence; I am not alone! O God, you have quieted my trembling heart.
Thank you, Father.

AMEN"

In the Introduction to this book I posed this question: *Does your commitment to Christ make a difference in your inner world?* In asking this question, I am in no way suggesting that Christ does not make a difference in our *outer world*. Of course he does! I can testify first-hand that Jesus makes a difference *both inside and out.* The home I was raised in qualifies for the label that we hear so often these days: *dysfunctional*. Mine was a moral home; my parents were not into alcohol, or drugs, or physical abuse. For that I am grateful. But my mother and father seemed not to care for each other. They fussed and fought till, as a little boy, my stomach tied itself in knots. Along with me, my three brothers and sister suffered pain as a result of our parents' animosity toward each other. Off and on, we attended church, but the roots of our faith did not grow deep. I felt certain my parents would eventually divorce. Before that could happen, my father died of a massive heart attack at the age of forty-six.

In contrast, my adult home has been one of the most loving families one could imagine. My kind and gentle wife, Mary Faith, is named after a missionary. She has been my friend and soul mate for forty years. We have two lovely daughters, two fine sons-in-law, and five of the most beautiful grandchildren on planet earth! Of course I am prejudiced, and proud of it! Mary Faith and I determined early on to center our lives in Christ and his church. Our children and their families are following the same path; for that we give thanks each day. I cannot put into words the difference that a loving Christian home has made for me—for our entire family. I hope and expect that generations to come will be blessed by the decision Mary Faith and I made to make Christ the Lord of our home.

☺ **Smile Awhile!**

Mary Mawmaw said to Adrian and Allison when they were toddlers, "I love you two!" Adrian responded, "I love you *one*!"

In the "Eye of the Storm"

However, the thrust of this devotional book is not so much the *outer life* as it is the *inner life*. Hence the question: *Does your commitment to Christ make a difference in your internal world?* Though my adult home has been filled with joy and harmony, life has not always been easy. Having come from a dysfunctional home, I have had to struggle at times with a lack of confidence, discouragement, and even depression. To be honest, I have spent a lifetime overcoming the wounds of my childhood. Additionally, a few years back, I experienced a severe illness which almost took my life. Mary Faith has become allergic to dust, pollen, and strong smells. As a third-grade teacher, her students are not allowed to wear perfume or cologne because of her allergic reactions. Her sense of smell has become so keen that I have teased, "The police are going to hire you to sniff-out drugs!" Though she has sought treatment for her allergies, she sometimes feels exhausted and anemic. Also, as minister and wife, we have dealt with difficult situations and people. Church life, as I'm sure you have discovered, can be enjoyable and positive as we connect with God and with our Christian brothers and sisters. But, as believers work through differences of opinion, church life can also be filled with stress and struggles. Even in a Christian community like the church, believers can hurt and be hurt.

The point being, that for everybody, *life is life* and people are people! As we move toward *a* more *gentle and simple life*, I just want readers to know that I don't write from a naive point of view. My family and I have not lived in a bubble, protected from the harsh realities of life. Like each of you, we yet have lessons to learn; school is still in session and will be till we die! Life has happened to us, *but Christ has also happened to us*, and that has made all the difference! How do people handle life without Jesus? Why would anyone want to face the ups and downs of life without the sustaining power, peace, and comfort that God provides? Who would want to face eternity without the hope that our faith brings? I wish everyone could know the joy and peace that comes in following Jesus. It troubles me when I see Christians who live *as though Christ never happened to them*! I am speaking of believers who live discouraged, anxious lives. They have not learned to process the ups and downs of life through eyes of faith. Here is the way the Apostle Paul describes life in Christ:

> Rejoice in the Lord always. I will say it again: Rejoice! [5] Let your gentleness be evident to all. The Lord is near. [6] Do not be anxious about anything, but in everything, by prayer and petition, with thanksgiving, present your requests to God. [7] And the peace of God, which transcends all understanding, will guard your hearts and your minds in Christ Jesus (Philip. 4:4-7).

Do Paul's words depict the way you live? If not, why not? All of us experience *shadow days* when we think the sun will never shine again. But Jesus is the Light of our world! After all, the "God who said, 'Let light shine out of darkness,' made his light shine in our hearts . . . in the face of Christ" (2 Cor. 4:6). Let's live in *the glow of that Eternal Flame!* In this quest for the fullest life, I sometimes slip and slide, fall backwards, and stumble forward. But my sights are set on the *abundant life* he promised, and I shall not settle for less. Nor should you! Our goal is to bring God our insufficiency, and, in return, receive *his all-sufficiency*.

"More Than Sufficient"

Not defending, but *depending;*
Not agitation, but *adoration;*
Not me, but *Thee;*
Not lust, but *love;*
Not greatness, but *faithfulness;*
Not might, but *meekness;*
Not ego, but *soul;*
Not power, but *peace.*
Oh, Wonderful God,
When I am tempted to say, "Not enough!"
Help me to realize that you are "More than sufficient!"

** A HUMOROUS INTERLUDE **

My gift: "It's a worm!"

A small congregation I served had a lady who was just a bit *unusual*. She was as sweet as could be, but not predictable. Once, while I was up front leading the singing, this lady approached me. She said, "I have a gift for your new grandson." Then she said, "It's his first worm!" I thanked her. After the services, my wife and I took her gift (in a paper cup) to the wastebasket. Inside was something wrapped in tinfoil; inside that, was something wrapped in a Kleenex. Under these layers we found a large, lively earthworm—who squirmed for freedom. Together my wife and I had a good chuckle. After all, as someone once said, "It's the thought that counts!"

A Faith-Shaped Purpose Statement

The path to a gentle and simple life begins with *a faith-shaped purpose statement.* I have already shared mine with you:

Today!
To live in a gentle and simple way;
To love, to learn, to laugh, to pray;
To live in a gentle and simple way;
Today!

Do you notice my purpose statement begins and ends with the word "Today"? That's because I have learned that I don't have the strength to live more than one day at a time. In the community where I ministered in Illinois, a country road crossed a small river via a bridge built some forty years earlier. Posted on either side of the bridge were signs which gave a specific weight limit for vehicles crossing the bridge; I think that the limit was ten tons. I always wondered what would happen if a heavier vehicle tried to cross the bridge; one day I found out. As I arrived at that juncture, the road was closed; a sign read: "Bridge Out." I enquired as to the circumstances and discovered that a large truck had ignored the warning sign and tried to cross the bridge anyway; it weighed much more than ten tons. The bridge collapsed throwing both truck and driver into the cold, dark river. Apparently the signs meant what they said!

"I Have Lived Today"

Happy the man, and happy he alone,
He who can call today his own.
He who, serene within, can say,
Tomorrow, do thy worst, for I have lived today.
(John Dryden)

I believe that God has placed a large sign in the sky to warn us of the "load" we can safely carry; that sign is called *the sun*. By establishing the natural cycle of the day, God has proclaimed: "Live one day at a time." Jesus said, "Each day has enough trouble of its own" (Matt. 6:34). That's an interesting way to say it, don't you think? Our Lord seems to be acknowledging that life is difficult, *but that we can handle our troubles, if we take God as our Companion and live one day at a time.* None of us is strong enough to hold up under the pressure of *yesterday, today, and tomorrow*! If we are consumed with regret and guilt, then we're toting *yesterday* on our back. Today, of course, will have its own burdens; count on it. Then, if we add *tomorrow's* anticipated *troubles*, we become loaded down with worry and anxiety; that's too much to carry. If we ignore God's sign in the sky, the *bridge* that is our life may well collapse! Even if the bridge does not totally break down, we still find ourselves overwhelmed—enduring a joyless existence, saturated with hurry, flurry, and worry. But it does not have to be that way! We can *learn* to make God-honoring, life-fulfilling choices—

one *day at a time*! I have always appreciated the way Thomas Carlyle described our task: "To shape the whole future is not our problem; but only to shape faithfully a small part of it, according to rules already known."

☺ **Smile Awhile!**

Miss Allison, age three: "Adventuresome" would be the word to describe Allison. She likes to *walk on the edge* (or is it, *run* on the edge!). Though she's only nine, she has broken her arm twice! We have a picture of her when she was two. In it, she's taking a rocking chair to its very limits—just for the *fun* of it! Once, when riding with grandma over a hilly road, Allison proclaimed with joy: "This is the Tick-Er-A-Tion part; it tickles my tummy!"

"David, remember that God has given you the gift of today. Don't spoil it; make wise choices." In addition to my purpose statement, I often begin my day with a list of what I call "focus thoughts" which help me quietly plan my day. Each day I want to:

- Stay centered in the Lord!
- Keep life simple.
- Treat everyone with kindness, including yourself.
- Nurture your soul.
- Take care of your body.

- Gently feed your mind.
- Focus on the good.
- Never hurry.
- Practice forgiveness.
- Laugh often.
- Hope always.
- Maintain perspective.
- Stay grateful.
- Cherish the Moment!

Prayer: A "Soulful Day"

"Lord, this has been a good day—a "soulful day." I could ask for no more: gentle work, a quiet lunch, an excellent supper by Mary Faith, a worship service, a time to exercise and watch the news, a good book, then a time to read Scripture, pray and hum some majestic hymns. Would you now grant a night of refreshing rest? Thank you, my God. In Jesus' Sweet Name. AMEN."

☺ **Smile Awhile!**

From Miss Adrian, age two: She was sitting on her cousin's lap when she noticed some small pock marks on Amy's face. Amy explained to Adrian that she retained the scars from having had chicken pox as a little girl. Adrian was quiet for a few seconds. Then she said to Amy: "You'd better stay away from those chickens!"

"Each Good Day"

My wife and I have enjoyed *The Lord of the Rings* trilogy by J. R. R. Tolkien. Long before the movies came out, we had read and reread the books about the small fictional beings called "hobbits." Frodo and his companion, Sam, struggle desperately to make the long, perilous journey into the very heart of evil, a place called *Mordor* with an evil Lord named *Sauron*. Several times along the way, it appears that Sam and Frodo will fail in their mission, that deadly, dark forces will actually overwhelm them. At one stage in their journey the hobbits reach a point of total exhaustion; they simply cannot continue. To their good fortune, they arrive at a wonderful place for rest and recovery that is called "Rivendell"; it is described as the "Last Homely Home East of the Sea." Listen to its description:

> "For a while the hobbits continued to talk and think of the past journey and of the perils that lay ahead; but such was the virtue of the land of Rivendell that soon all fear and anxiety was lifted from their minds. The future, good or ill, was not forgotten, but ceased to have any power over the present. Health and hope grew strong in them, and they were content with each good day as it came, taking pleasure in every meal, and in every word and song."

At Rivendell, the hobbits "were content with *each good day* as it came." Would you not love to live *in such a way, in such a place*? I believe that the closer we live to the Lord, the closer we will come to our own personal "Rivendell." To so live, we must not only cultivate an awareness of God's presence; we must also live in the *bloom of the present moment.* I am describing the life I believe God intended for his children. It is a life overflowing with love, laughter, peace and prayer, where "each good day" is enjoyed as it comes. Don't misunderstand; I am not proposing a pretend world of perpetual ease and comfort. The external world of chaos will not go away; the storms of life will continue to rage. But we will change on the inside, as we surrender control to God. Consider the example of the Apostle Paul. In the midst of *this world*, with all its horrendous evils, Paul lived in gratitude, contentment, and God's peace. The path I lay out is consistent with the Apostle's description: "We are hard pressed on every side, but not crushed; perplexed, but not in despair; [9] persecuted, but not abandoned; struck down, but not destroyed" (2 Cor. 4:8-9). I don't think anyone can top Paul's life purpose statement: "For to me, to live is Christ and to die is gain" (Phil 1:21).

A reminder: Don't be surprised by my "Humorous Interludes" along the way; in this volume we will laugh our way forward—"one good day" at a time! Together we will grow as we learn to enjoy *each good day.* I am not sure who wrote the following piece, but its wisdom is undeniable.

Yesterday is History;
Tomorrow is Mystery;
Today is *Gift*:
That's why they call it "*The Precious Present*!"

Prayer: A Gift Called TODAY!

"Father, You have given me a gift called 'TODAY.' What a precious gift. I know it won't be a perfect day—you never said it would be so. I may face a variety of difficult situations that are beyond my control, but not beyond yours! Lord, I cannot carry the burdens of yesterday and tomorrow; if I try, I won't have strength for today. Thank you, Lord, that you give me my 'daily bread.' In Jesus' name. AMEN."

☺ **Smile Awhile!**

Katy, age two: Katy always sang and twirled about on her tiptoes. She usually sang, "I've got the Joy, Joy, Joy, Joy down in my heart." One day on the playground as she was climbing, her mommy heard her singing, "Happy, Happy, Happy, Happy!" over and over again.

** A HUMOROUS INTERLUDE **

My First Funeral: The day I lost a funeral procession *I was leading*!

A young minister has much to learn as he adjusts to all of the various responsibilities of the ministry. Though he has been taught to preach funerals, perform weddings and baptisms, still he must learn by experiencing these events. I remember well my first funeral, some thirty-five years ago; it was on that occasion I lost a funeral procession that I was leading!

The funeral was held in a small Illinois town close to a church I had served only a month. I wasn't actually preaching, but rather assisting an older, established minister as he preached the funeral for a deceased gentleman from my congregation. I read Scripture and had prayer. After the service, the procession was to go from the funeral home to the church, which was a distance of about seven miles. Often the minister will lead the funeral procession in his automobile. The older minister, in a effort to be kind since it was my congregation, insisted that I lead the funeral procession. With some fear and misgivings, I agreed to do so. There was a policeman on a motorcycle out in front of me leading us out of this small town. It was a comfort to have him show me the way, as I realized the Police officer was taking us on a route that I had not traveled before. About two miles out of town, he stopped his motorcycle, stopped traffic, and pointed me to turn left on a particular road. I suddenly realized that I was leading a funeral procession to the church, but I had no idea of my location! I did my best to guess my way to the church building. Suddenly, I looked in my rear view mirror, and the funeral procession was gone! They had turned on a road that I had not even noticed. Obviously, this was a very embarrassing situation. My wife was in the car with me. We had to find our way to the church building so that the service could be concluded; people were waiting! But we did not know where we were, or which of those country roads to take! We did our best, but still, it took us a half an hour or so (or was it ten hours?), to find the church. Finally, the service was concluded—with the assistance of a red-faced young minister! To this day I refuse to allow my vehicle to be first in a funeral procession. It will never happen to me again!

Chapter Two

The Ups and the Downs

Beside Quiet Waters

I cannot count the number of times over the years I have turned to Psalm 23 for strength in time of need. It comforts me that through the ups and downs we have a Shepherd who leads us across the dangerous and jagged terrain we call life. I especially appreciate these words from Psalm 23: "He makes me to lie down in green pastures, he leads me by quiet waters, he restores my soul" (Psalm 23:2). Is anything more beautiful than a quiet lake in the evening when it reflects the myriad colors of a brilliant sunset? Notice that the Psalmist said, ". . . he restores my soul." Why would we need to have our souls restored? Well, sometimes the waters are not still, but rolling and churning. Consider these verses from Psalm 22: "I am poured out like water, and all my bones are out of joint. My heart has turned to wax; it has melted away within me. [15] My strength is dried up like a potsherd, and my tongue sticks to the roof of my mouth; you lay me in the dust of death" (Psalm 22:14-15). Living a gentle and simple life demands the kind of honesty with God we see in the Psalms. How thankful I am for these psalmists who laid bare their souls. It helps me to know that they faced the ups and downs of the human roller coaster, yet relied always on our Faithful God. Sometimes they fussed with him and cried out against perceived injustice, but always they trusted him. I give thanks for the Good Shepherd who leads me by quiet waters. Sometimes *I need my soul restored,* and I am guessing you would say the same. It helps me to express my needs to God poetically, as I did in "Beside Quiet Waters."

A trickling brook;
Then a churning stream!

A gently flowing river;
Then a torrent of twisting liquid!

Gentle, rhythmic, waves lapping inward and receding;
Suddenly, crashing walls of relentless energy;
Boulders crushed to grains of sand!

Tiny raindrops falling from a leaden sky;
Then houses and barns ripped from their foundations
and shattered by the raging flood!

"He leads me beside quiet waters."

Psalm 23 encourages us; it also presents an honest depiction of life. Consider these additional observations which are both explicit and implicit in Psalm 23:

- He guides us in "paths of righteousness" (23:3). If so, there must be dangerous paths of *unrighteousness* to be avoided.

- His "rod and staff" comfort us; at times we desperately need that consolation (23:4).

- We have to deal with people who don't like us, for he "prepares a table before us in the presence of our enemies" (23:5).

- Some day we will all traverse "the valley of the shadow of death." But thankfully, as we tread through that dark valley, he is right there beside us to give us hope and courage ("for you are with me"; Psalm 23:4).

<u>The Ups and Downs</u>

The Psalms overflow with the "stuff of life." If we read them thoughtfully and prayerfully, we will see the joy and sorrow, the hurts and healings that define our earthly existence. Most of all, we see our Father God who is Lord of the ups and the downs. That's what I entitled my prayer: "Lord of the Ups and the Downs!"

"Lord, we are on a never ending roller-coaster!

Up, then down!

Down, then up!

Up. Up. Up.

Down. Down. Down.

Then Down!

Then Up!

Up, up, down, down, down, up!

You, O God, are Lord of the Ups and the Downs.
Father, I know we need the ups and the downs.
If we had only the *ups*, we would remain small,
self-centered, even arrogant.
If we had only the *downs*, we would be hopeless,
disheartened, even discouraged.
So, I claim You as Lord of the Ups and the Downs.
And I await the final

UP!"

"**Surely goodness and love will follow me all the days of my life, and I will dwell in the house of the Lord forever**" (Psalm 23:6).

☺ **Smile Awhile!**

Mr Andrew, age two: At eighteen months, his mommy was putting him to bed. He slipped from her hands and fell a few inches to the mattress. She exclaimed, "Oh, I dropped you on your head!" Andrew started laughing and saying, "Drop you on your head!" Now, every night, when his mommy puts him to bed, Andrew says, "Drop you on head!" and Crystal must drop him a few short inches to the mattress. Every night he goes to bed laughing!

Who's in Control?

It is impossible to live a gentle and simple life unless we are willing *to trust completely our Mighty God*. A word that we humans don't use often is the word "control." I've never heard anyone say, "I want to *control* you!" But I have seen lots of people who try to control others! Also, I have never heard anyone say, "My life is under *my control*!" But I have seen lots of folks who live as though that were true. Believe me, *life cannot be controlled*, and the only thing you get by trying is headaches and ulcers! In his Epistle, James warns us against the presumptuous approach that assumes life will go on according to our perceived plan: "Now listen, you who say, 'Today or tomorrow we will go to this or that city, spend a year there, carry on business and make money.' [14] Why, you do not even know what will happen tomorrow. What is your life? You are a mist that appears for a little while and then vanishes" (James 4:13-14). To live as though the future is guaranteed and predictable is the essence of presumption; to leave God out of our plans brings disaster!

"But Life Said"

(DAE)

"I'll live in a mansion, just you wait and see!"
But she lives in a mobile home—ten feet by thirty-three!

Before he was thirty he said, "I'll be rich!"
That was before he pulled the wrong switch!

"Someday," she said, "I'll own that big lot!"
But all she got was a six by six plot!

When asked about the Lord, he never gave an answer,
Then the doctor said, "I'm afraid it's cancer!"

"One day," she said, "I'll drive a big, fancy car!"
But she drives an old-junker than won't go far!

She proclaimed: "Just like my grandma, I'll live to one-hundred-and-three!"
But they buried her at thirty-seven under the old apple tree!

"Look around you!" he said, "all this land is *my homestead*!"
But then came the accident; now he lives in his bed.

The point being, when we try to predict the future, we only make a mess of things. "Control freaks" (which includes all of us at times!) need to *learn to surrender control to God. No surrender*? Then, *no serenity*! Whatever pain, sadness, or heartache encumbers you, give it up to God. Whatever worry or frustration haunts the inner recesses of your heart, give them up to God. I am not suggesting that we refuse to take responsibility for our problems—only *that we leave the final solution to our Father*. His shoulders can bear the load; ours cannot. God told Isaiah: "As the heavens are higher than the earth, so are my ways higher than your ways and my thoughts than your thoughts" (Isaiah 55:9). *The simple life demands that we surrender control to God!* After all, he "is able to do immeasurably more than all we ask or imagine, according to his power that is at work within us" (Eph. 3:20) That's why Paul wrote of God: "to him be glory in the church and in Christ Jesus throughout all generations, for ever and ever! Amen" (Eph. 3:21). Remind yourself daily: "We have a *God who is able!*"

Prayer: Trying Too Hard

"Lord, I am doing it again; I am trying too hard. It's like I have to prove myself, rather than simply accepting that my life is under your control. As a result, I feel exhausted, over-extended. I come in these quiet moments to confess my sin and submit myself anew to your sovereign will. In Christ's name. AMEN."

☺ Smile Awhile!

Allison, age two: As Allison approached baby twin goats in her great-grandparents' field, the two goats moved away from her. She eased her way forward with her hand held out and said, "I LOVE YOU GOATS! I GOOD. I NO MONSTER!"

<u>Lifting "HEAVY"</u>

David: "Man! This is heavy! What a load! In fact, I think I will just call it *HEAVY*! Now, what am I going to do with it? Something must be done. I am about to be crushed under the load! I know I can find a solution. I can! HEAVY! HEAVY! HEAVY! My heart is racing; my head is aching; my soul is burdened. In every direction, all I see is HEAVY!"

The Lord: "David, what do you have there?"

David: "Oh, nothing, really, Lord. This is just a problem I have to solve; this is just HEAVY. I'm working on it; the solution is almost at hand. I am exhausted, but I will struggle on; I must solve HEAVY!"

The Lord: "David, I notice that you use the 'I' word a lot! Is that your favorite word?"

David: "Pardon, Lord, I didn't quite hear that. I'm just so busy and burdened with HEAVY."

The Lord: "David, do you really think you can carry that by yourself?"

David: "Well, Lord, I admit that I often feel overwhelmed with HEAVY. But I can deal with it. Besides, there's really no one else to help me!"

The Lord: "David, did you ever stop to think that *I might be able* to help you? After all, I have been dealing with HEAVY for untold generations."

David: "You, Lord? Ask you to help me with HEAVY? But you are so busy Lord, and HEAVY is *my problem*!"

The Lord: "Do you think I am ever too busy to help my children?"

David: "No, Lord; I wouldn't think that!"

The Lord: "Do you think that I don't care when you have a problem like HEAVY?"

David: "I know you care, Lord."

The Lord: "David, if you know that I care, why are you trying to carry HEAVY by yourself?"

The Lord: "Don't answer that question. Rather, just think about it and pray about it. Now David, stand aside, and let me see what I can do!"

David: "Wow, HEAVY is gone!"

The Lord: "You sound surprised. Let me ask you another question."

David: "Of course, Lord, anything!"

The Lord: "David, don't you read your Bible? Or, perhaps you read it, *but don't believe it*?"

Prayer: Our Weakness

"Lord, to you we would bring our burdens. You take our soiled and tattered threads, and weave them into a garment more beautiful than we could ever imagine. You take our fear, and make it a powerful faith that moves mountains. You take our anxiety, and transform it into a peace that passes all understanding. You take our cynicism and discouragement, and turn them into hearts overflowing with grace and gratitude. You take our weakness, our sickness, our vulnerability, and make us satisfied with the sufficiency of your grace. Most of all, you give us the gift of your Holy Presence. What a Mighty God you are! AMEN."

☺ Smile Awhile!

Andrew, age one: Adrian, Allison, and Andrew have a little dog named Oreo. One day Andrew was standing right beside me; suddenly he was gone! Then I realized, he had crawled into Oreo's cage, and shut the door! Said his mommy: "He likes it in there; he will often crawl in and sit for a while to have a little privacy."

** A HUMOROUS INTERLUDE **

"Breathe on me, Johnny! Breathe on me!"

My wife, Mary Faith, has been an elementary school teacher for twenty-six years. She teaches in a small, rural school in the foothills of the Smoky Mountains. She could write a book on her experiences. Once, when passing the kindergarten classroom, she heard the strangest thing. The children were all saying: "Breathe on me, Johnny! Breathe on me!" These comments were followed by great gushes of breath which sounded like someone blowing out candles on a birthday cake. Mary Faith poked her head in to see what was going on. She learned that Johnny had just discovered he had chickenpox, and his teacher had gone to call his mother so she could pick him up. The other children were hoping for such good fortune themselves. They were all saying, "Breathe on me, Johnny!" He was doing his best!

☺ **Smile Awhile!**

Mr Andrew, age two: Oreo, the family dog, had always liked to be close to Andrew, but now seemed to be avoiding him. Mommy wondered why and finally solved the puzzle. Andrew had learned that he could throw, and his favorite projectiles were *blocks*; unfortunately, *his favorite target was Oreo*! His mommy took him on her lap and explained that the blocks hurt Oreo. If he did it again, mommy would spank. Andrew slid off her lap grinning mischievously; he then proceeded to pick up another block and throw it at Oreo. After several firm corrections, Andrew learned that he was going to have to quit this particular form of target practice!

Chapter Three

My Will and God's Will

Putting the First, first

Almost every time I find myself overly stressed, frustrated, and discouraged, it's because I've failed to submit myself to God's will, choosing rather to be guided by my own self-centered instincts. This book is about learning to live gentle, simple lives. Among other things, that means living as persons of the *soul,* as opposed to persons of the *ego*. I once saw ego defined as "Edging God Out." Each day I must ask myself this question: "Am I living to do God's will, or am I living to do my will?" If we are to live as a people of the soul, and not a people of the ego, we must learn to put the First, first. That is, each day, we must align our priorities and be sure that we put God first. Jesus said it like this, "But seek first his kingdom and his righteousness and all these things will be given to you as well" (Matt. 6:33). In God's kingdom, the King comes first! The Devil doesn't say, "Take the Lord completely off your list; pretend he is not there!" The Evil One whispers in your ear: "Just move the Lord down to second place so you will have space for yourself!" That, my friends, is a recipe for a life of chaos and spiritual disaster! To live a life of gentleness and simplicity, we must win the nearest battle; it takes place in our hearts. Vernard Eller says it like this: “The ‘first’ of the simple life must be a single-willed centering upon God; there is absolutely no room for variation on this point” (*The Simple Life*). Every day, as I search the depths of my soul, I must ask myself, “Have I considered God’s will, or put my will before his?”

Jesus said: "Love the Lord your God with all your heart and with all your soul and with all your mind” (Matt. 22:37). As this command appears in Deut. 6:5, the word “might” appears as opposed to “mind.” The meaning, of course, remains unchanged: “Love God *with your whole person*.” Jesus calls this “the *first* and the *greatest* commandment.” He then adds the second, “Love your neighbor as yourself” (Matt. 22:38). The *essence* of the simple life is to love God and to acknowledge yourself as loved by God. The “essence” of anything is its “inner nature.” When everything that’s unimportant or peripheral is removed, what’s left is *the essence*. What is the simple life about? It’s about *internalizing God’s love* and *loving God in return with your whole being*. Then, *do all you can to pass that love on to others*. Notice that you look away from yourself (to God and others) to find yourself. Joy, peace, and contentment are byproducts. That is, they come unbidden *when we focus our lives on God and others.* A life focused on one’s self is complicated and frustrating; the ego keeps getting in the way of gentleness and simplicity.

Prayer: Done With Lesser Things

"Father, let me be done with lesser things. I am astounded by your love for me as revealed in the death of your Son on the cross for my sins. Let me return that love to you with full devotion. As your love flowed down to me, may my love flow up to you. As your love flows to me, may it flow through me to others. In Christ's name. Amen."

☺ Smile Awhile!

Adrian, age four: David Pawpaw put a clothes basket on his head, crawled around on the floor, and pretended to be a gorilla. The girls fed him through holes in the basket, and Allison put a cup under it for the gorilla's food. After Pawpaw left the room and came back as himself, Adrian said, "You were a good gorilla, but you were a little bit wild!"

"Filled to the measure!"

Someone once wrote, "The winds of grace are always blowing, but we must put up our sails." Early in my Christian walk I had a hard time believing that God loved me and had forgiven my sins. Though the winds of grace were blowing, I had difficulty "putting up my sails." Because I fought that battle, I sympathize with those who struggle in a similar manner. Sometimes *grace* seems too good to be true! The change came for me when I finally took my eyes off myself and began to focus on Jesus. The following verses are some of my favorite in all of Scripture. If you have trouble accepting the fact that God loves you, I encourage you to read them every day; let your heart be fully persuaded.

> And I pray that you, being rooted and established in love, may have power, together with all the saints, to grasp how wide and long and high and deep is the love of Christ, and to know this love that surpasses knowledge—that you may be filled to the measure of all the fullness of God. (Eph. 3:17-21).

When are we filled to the fullness of God? *When we know how deeply he loves us*! In my prayer journal I expressed this poetically in a piece I entitled, "Filled to the Measure."

"Filled to the measure"
What a great treasure!
God's love, how wide and long and high and deep!
Covered by his tender mercies—even when we sleep!
Rooted and established in his gentle love,
Showered with mercy from heaven above,
Such love no mind can conceive.

But through Jesus, God says, "Receive!"
There on Calvary, he died in our place.
We are made righteous by his infinite grace.
Before this divine love we bow, yielded and still.
As obedient children, we surrender our will.
"Filled to the measure!"
What a great treasurer!

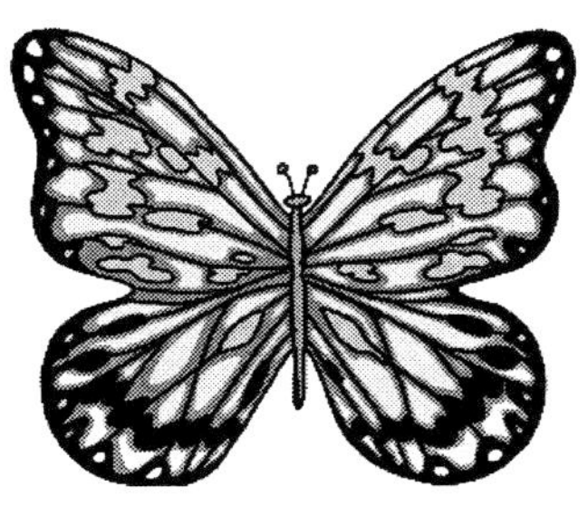

☺ **Smile Awhile!**

Allison, age four: We had just taken the girls to see a children's movie at the mall, and were walking through the food court. With joyful abandonment, Allison skipped and swung her arms about. She said, "My other grandma says I'm an angel, but *I'm a butterfly*. I'm flying!!! I look like I'm walking, but I'm flying!"

☺ Smile Awhile!

Miss Katy, age three: Katy tells her mommy that when she grows up she is going to have fourteen children! She loves to hang out clothes in her room for each of the fourteen. She also has some names picked out: "Uddy"; "Fuddy"; Suddy"; "Duddy"; "Rainbow"; and "Sleepy!"

"When You See Me?"

I love the words of the hymn written by Julia H. Johnston: "Marvelous grace of our loving Lord . . . Grace that is greater than all our sin!" Those who have heard me speak have almost certainly heard me say, "You can't count until you can say, 'one-two-three.' You can't read until you can say, 'a-b-c.' You can't sing until you can say, 'Do-re-mi.' Furthermore, *you don't begin to live* until you can say, '*JESUS LOVES ME*!'" Never lose the wonder of his grace at work in you: "Though your sins are like scarlet, they shall be as white as snow; though they are red as crimson, they shall be like wool" (Isaiah 1:18).

Think of our Lord's encounter with the "woman at the well" (John 4). What a mess she had made of her life. Jesus said to her: "The fact is, you have had five husbands, and the man you now have is not your husband" (John 4:18). Many men had wanted her body, but none seemed to truly care about her as a person. She came *alone* to the well at noon—

probably because the respectable women would not be seen with her. The woman at the well is a study in paradox:

- She had water, but was thirsty.
- She had many lovers, but ached to be loved.
- She was surrounded by people, but felt a profound loneliness.
- She knew all about religion, but she knew little of the Savior.

When this woman first encountered Jesus, she must have thought, "Here comes another one; I know what he wants!" But as she spoke with Jesus, her eyes were opened, her heart captivated by the Lover Of Her Soul. By Jesus' love, this lonely, lost woman was transformed. After a lifetime of horrendous thirst, she drank the living water and would never thirst again. I reflected on this transformed person in a piece I entitled, "When You See Me?"

"What do you see when you see me?"
(DAE)

Hurting and lonely and empty inside,
Painful feelings I had learned to hide.

"What do you see when you see me?"

I was not a person, but only a shell,
Living in my own sin-shaped hell.

I had spent a lifetime learning to pretend,

Hiding the aching loneliness within.

"What do you see when you see me?"

Then I met a man—so different was He;
He saw a "God-loved person" when he looked at me.

I knew he was different when I gazed in his face;
Then from his cup I drank the living water of grace.

In my wretched life, I had never known such love;
Now I had no doubt: *This was the Savior sent from above*!

"NOW, WHAT DO YOU SEE WHEN YOU SEE ME"?

Submission: To Please Him

The simple life then, is about accepting God's love for you and returning that love. The word which best describes that process for me is *submission*. It's a word disdained by our secular culture, which is mesmerized by *wealth*, *power,* and *fame*. In order to be a part of God's kingdom, we must submit ourselves to the King; we must put the First, first. We must make it our goal to please him in all we say and do. It pleases him when we accept his love for us and acknowledge that he has forgiven our sins. It pleases him when we love him *above all else*. It also pleases him when, in both word and deed, we share his love with others. Paul wrote: "So we make it our goal to please him, whether we are at home in the body or away from it" (2 Cor. 5:9). Is it then, our supreme desire to please him?

"Father, I Would Please You.
This Lord, is my utmost desire;
It burns within me like a fire.
I would please you.
This is the water that quenches my thirst,
In all I do, to put you first.
I would please you.
This is food for my hungry soul,
Only then do I feel whole.
My God, I would please you."

My Will and His Will

Note the comparison below that shows the difference between living to please myself and living to please God. If life is to be gentle and simple, *his will must come before my will.*

Living by "My Will"	**Living by "God's Will"**
Gratifying the Ego	Feeding the Soul
Feeling Empty & Unloved	Overwhelmed by Grace
Self	God/Christ/Others
Hurry/Worry/Flurry	Patient Acceptance & Gentle Effort
Complexity	Simplicity
Self Righteousness	God's Imputed Righteousness
Neurotic Perfection	Grace
Dissatisfaction	Contentment

An Inward Stillness

When we are able to acknowledge and accept God's love, a powerful transformation takes place inside of us. We no longer feel driven to prove ourselves to others. It's not that we believe we a have arrived. Rather, we learn to *trust the process* as God works in us. I like to say it in this manner: "Lord, I thank you for the person you have made me, and, for the person you are making me." An inner healing takes place as we allow God to take control. Another of my favorite verses in Scripture comes from Jude 1:21. It says simply, "Keep yourself in God's love as you wait for the mercy of our Lord Jesus Christ to bring you to eternal life." Henry Wadsworth Longfellow spoke of our surrender to God in a piece called "Singleness of Heart."

Let us then labor for an inward stillness,
An inward stillness and an inward healing,
That perfect silence where the lips and heart
Are still, and we no longer entertain
Our own imperfect thought and vain opinions,
But God alone speaks in us, and we wait
In singleness of heart, that we may know
His will, and the silence of our spirits,
That we may do His will, and do that only!

Prayer: My Only Real Temptation

"Dear Lord, My only real temptation is to doubt your love, to think of myself as beyond the reach of your love, to remove myself from the healing radiance of your love. To do these things is to move into the darkness of despair. Out of your love I came to life; by your love I am sustained, and to your love I am always called back. There are days of sadness and days of joy; there are feelings of guilt and feelings of gratitude; there are moments of failure and moments of success; but all of them are embraced by your unwavering love. AMEN." (By Henry Nouwen).

☺ Smile Awhile!

Katy, age three: "Mommy, Pawpaw loves me! He told me when I was a baby."

Chapter Four

Something and Nothing

Making Myself "Something"

From a slightly different perspective, this chapter reinforces the message of the last. If our lives are to be lived in a manner that is gentle and simple, we must allow God to set the agenda. If my energies are invested in building "Satan's kingdom" (often disguised as "my kingdom"), I simply cannot experience the abundant life. When my wishes and desires gravitate to the top of the list, I find myself shocked by the realization that I am building "David's kingdom" for "David's glory" and not God's kingdom for God's glory.

From a worldly perspective, what makes you "something"? Is it not: money? power? fame? beauty? success? When we are consumed by the pursuit of any of these, *we are building our own kingdom, not God's.* Our wants and desires become elevated above those of our Lord. Remember, we must keep the First, first! What do you put at the top of the list when you are busy about the business of building your *own kingdom*, making yourself into *something*? Let me tell you what goes to the top of *my* list: productivity, control, recognition, and success.

It shames me to think of the time I have spent trying to make myself into "something"! Let me list some of the questions that take over my mind when I am building "David's kingdom." Perhaps similar thoughts occasionally inhabit the dark recesses of your mind.

- What do other people think about me?
- Am I a success?
- Did they like my sermon?
- How do I compare with other speakers and writers?
- Are my students impressed with how much I know?
- Are people reading my books?
- Am I productive?
- Will this book be a success?

When we start to play these worldly games within ourselves, there is little chance that we can live calm, peaceful lives. Instead, we are driven, compulsive, and competitive; we begin to view others as adversaries, as opposed to friends.

When I begin to ask questions like those mentioned above, I know that Satan has gained a foothold in my heart. Indeed, I am bounded on the east, the west, the north, and the south by David! That's scary! Jesus Christ is no longer my model for thinking and living. Hear the words of our Lord: "If anyone would come after me, he must deny himself and take up his cross and follow me. [35] For whoever wants to save his life will lose it, but whoever loses his life for me and for the gospel will save it" (Mark 8:34-36). May I, with caution, paraphrase the message I believe our Father was giving us? "Quit trying to make yourself into somebody special; imitate my Son who made himself *nothing*!" I don't know about you, but the more time I spend thinking about myself, the more miserable I am! Even worse, the farther I find myself from a life that is gentle and simple. I like the way Vernard Eller says it: "Consider dropping any remaining pretenses of being sophisticated, all-knowing, better or worse than anyone else. Be just who you are at the moment, and stop dragging around all those cardboard cutouts of your imaginary pseudo-selves."

Each day I want to love, learn, laugh, and pray. All four of these disciplines have one central purpose: to center my life on God, not on David! I long for the day when I can honestly say with Paul: "I have been crucified with Christ and I no longer live, but Christ lives in me" (Gal. 2:20). Is it any wonder that the Apostle Paul could sing hymns while sitting in a jail cell?

Jesus "Emptied Himself"

Listen to Paul: "Your attitude should be the same as that of Christ Jesus: [6] Who, being in very nature God, did not consider equality with God something to be grasped, [7] but made himself nothing, taking the very nature of a servant" (Philip. 2:5-7). Think about it! God's Son "emptied himself" and made himself "nothing." From a worldly perspective, Jesus was not interested in making himself *something*. When the

Evil One tempted Jesus in a Judean desert, he did his best to get our Lord to bypass God's way (the cross!) and instead to make a name for himself (Matt. 4:1-11). The devil wanted Jesus to use his supernatural powers for his own glory: "If you are the Son of God, tell these stones to become bread" (Matt. 4:3). If I might paraphrase the second temptation: "Throw yourself down from the highest point on the temple; after all, the angels will not allow you to be injured, and *people will be impressed*!" (Matt. 4:6). Finally, Satan offered to give Jesus all "the kingdoms of the world"—if only he would fall down and worship him. In every temptation, Jesus steadfastly refused the voice of the Tempter, and admonished him: "Away from me, Satan! For it is written: 'Worship the Lord your God, and serve him only'" (Matt. 4:10).

The Kingdom of Jesus

In the Garden of Eden, the serpent tempted Eve: "For God knows that when you eat of it your eyes will be opened, and you will be like God, knowing good and evil" (Gen. 3:5). All men, I believe, are tempted to become, not simply *like God*, but *to become God*. As I indicated earlier, my wife and I are fans of J. R. R. Tolkien and *The Lord of the Rings* trilogy. In this fictional saga,

Frodo and his companion, Sam, make a perilous journey to *Mordor.* There Frodo must throw the *ring of power* into a lake of fire before Sauron recovers it and uses it to consolidate his wicked control over all the earth. Every character who comes near the ring, including Frodo and Sam, is tempted to take the ring for his own, and thus become the one supreme power who rules the world. In Tolkien's fiction, the evil "ring" of power is described in this manner:

In the land of Mordor where the Shadows lie.
One Ring to rule them all, One ring to find them,
One Ring to bring them all and in the darkness
bind them
In the Land of Mordor where the Shadows lie.

The Scriptures teach us that there are two kingdoms which vie for our single-willed allegiance. The Dark Lord (Satan) seduces us to reject God's Kingdom and King, and devote ourselves wholly to his evil cause. He whispers to us as he did to Eve: "You really want to become like God, don't you?" No one can live a peaceful and simple life if their heart is captured by a secular culture where *self is the center of everything* and *evil fills men's hearts*. The Apostle Paul persistently warned that the "god of this age" is able to blind the mind so that we "cannot see the light of the gospel of the glory of Christ, who is the image of God" (2 Cor. 4:4).

The point is, we cannot expect to enjoy the presence and peace of God if we have already given our hearts to the Lord of Darkness. If Jesus made himself *nothing*, should we spend much time making ourselves *something*? Remember, this is war! Satan will do anything in his power to corrupt the hearts of men and draw them away from their Creator! The wily serpent of Eden wants us obsessively concerned with ourselves, always striving to make a name for ourselves—to become "something." Only absolute allegiance to the God of heaven and to his Son Jesus Christ will protect us from the schemes of the Evil One. Said Jesus, "No one can serve two masters. Either he will hate the one and love the other, or he will be devoted to the one and despise the other" (Matt. 6:24). The following verse I entitled, "One Lord!"

In the Kingdom of Jesus where no Shadows lie.
One Lord to rule them all, One Savior to find them,
One God to save them all and from Satan's grip unbind them
In the Kingdom of Jesus where no Shadows lie.

"He made himself nothing"

Who are your heroes? Who do you admire? Is there a particular actor or actress? Perhaps a skilled sports figure? I admit that I would like to hit a golf ball like Tiger Woods! But in truth, all the heroes and heroines of this world leave me disappointed and empty. While they may be skilled and famous, all too often their private lives are confused and chaotic. Many have made a total mess of life—yet, they are admired and imitated! My only *real hero* is Jesus. His selfless love and sacrificial life influence me beyond all others. Therefore, I want to be conformed to the image of Christ. I willingly accept the label that Jesus wore: "nothing" (Philip. 2:7). I reflected on *my Hero* when I wrote the piece entitled, "King Nothing!"

"King Nothing!"

They came; quite exquisite—all three.
They came escorted by "nothing."
"nothing" pointed each to a royal seat
trimmed in purple.
Their names were "WEALTH," "POWER," and
"FAME."
How glorious each looked in royal garb.
Having seated them properly, "nothing" sat
upon the floor.
Tonight!
Tonight!
ONE would be crowned KING!
"WEALTH?" "POWER?" or "FAME?"
Electricity filled the air…
The whole earth held it's breath …
Only ONE could be chosen KING.
The ROYAL CHOOSER would point his finger,
and it would be done;

HE would be the ONE.
The ROYAL FINGER moved and rested ...
Upon "WEALTH!"
"'Tis done," said some.
"nothing" prepared to place the crown upon
WEALTH...
but then the ROYAL FINGER MOVED AGAIN.
This time 'twas "POWER" that would wear the crown!
But no!
Again the ROYAL FINGER moved.
For sure the choice was made;
"FAME" would be KING!
The ROYAL CHOOSER moved again
And came to rest ...
All sat stunned;
It could not be!
But it was!
The ROYAL FINGER stopped on ...
"nothing!"
"nothing?"

KING "nothing"?
Yes!
Yes!
Only "nothing" could wear the crown!
"KING NOTHING"!

** A HUMOROUS INTERLUDE **

"Where's my cane?"

For thirteen years my wife and I have led worship services in the community room of a government subsidized housing project called Summit Tower Apartments. During the week, I am a professor at Johnson Bible College. In the worship service, I direct the music and preach; my wife plays the piano. We have grown to love these people deeply. Because of age and health concerns, most residents of the Towers are unable to travel to their own churches. Our attendance at worship is never very large; we average less than twenty. Wheelchairs and "walkers" are common; the congregation is not able to stand when we sing or pray. I sometimes playfully tell them that we are going to sponsor a race down the hallway to see who has the fastest wheelchair! God has given us this little flock to serve, and we feel blessed with this opportunity. My wife and I do what we can to make their lives cheerful. We give them little gifts at Christmas, Easter, and Mother's Day. We call on them when they are in the hospital. Over the years, I have preached many funerals for our small congregation.

After service one Sunday a lady in her eighties exclaimed, "Where's my cane? I can't go anywhere without my cane!" Another lady answered her question: "You didn't bring it with you this morning!"

Too Ambitious

(By Elizabeth Barrett Browning, Aurora Leigh)

I was too ambitious in my deed,
And thought to outdistance all men in success
Till God came on me, marked the place, and said:
"Illdoer, henceforth keep within this line,
Attempting less than others"—and I stand
And work among Christ's little ones, content.

Prayer: To Empty Myself

"Father, I don't want to pattern my life after those living to build their own kingdom. I long, with all I have and am, to be crucified to myself that Christ might live in me. I don't want to be motivated by ambition, greed, or envy. Like Jesus, I want to empty myself and become a servant. Always and ever my God, I would live and die to build your Kingdom, not mine. I come anew to dedicate myself to that purpose; I want to bring glory and honor to your Great Name. AMEN."

Chapter Five

A Good Day and a Bad Day

The Capacity to Choose

Victor Frankl authored a wonderful little book entitled *Man's Search For Meaning*. In that book, Frankl asserts "the greatest of all freedoms is the freedom to choose one's attitude." During the course of any given day, circumstances occur over which we have no control. Bad things happen to all of us. However, each of us has the capacity *to choose our response*. Of all living creatures, man alone has the power to *interpret*. Each day contains enough good to make us *happy*; there's also enough evil, frustration, and unfairness in each day to make us *miserable*! But remember, we are able to choose our focus and *interpret*! Have you trained yourself to see the good, the beautiful, and the positive? Or have you have trained yourself to see the bad, the ugly, and the negative? Most often this day (this life!) will be exactly what we choose to make it. In my journal, I once wrote: "David, today you have everything you need to make you happy, and more. All you have to do is *choose wisely*."

I am suggesting, then, that we make each day good or bad, according to our own choices. Contentment is a conscious choice. Apart from Jesus, no one seems to have understood this better, than the

Apostle Paul. In Philippians 4:12, Paul wrote, "I know what it is to be in need, and I know what it is to have plenty. I have learned the secret of being content in any and every situation, whether well fed or hungry, whether living in plenty or in want." Paul wrote those words from a jail cell. Yet, if the reader did not know that fact, he would think the Apostle a man without a care in the world. Earlier I quoted Paul in Philippians: "Rejoice in the Lord always, I will say it again, rejoice. Let your gentleness be evident to all. The Lord is near. Do not be anxious about anything, but in everything, by prayer and petition, with thanksgiving, present your requests to God" (Philip. 4:4-6). I believe Paul meant every word that he wrote. I am convinced that, though he sat in a prison cell, his heart was filled with joy, thanksgiving, and peace. Paul trusted God; he accepted life on its own terms because *God was in control*. Whatever the day brought, good or bad, Paul was determined to process those circumstances through eyes of faith. With full confidence in God, he became thoroughly and completely content.

A Bad Day?

Edith has had a really bad day—or has she? It all started when she learned that she would have to make a trip to the doctor. As she put on her favorite dress, a button popped off. She called a cab, and asked that she be taken to the doctor's office. After they arrived, the cab driver charged her too much. Then, when she complained, the cab driver got angry and said some unkind words. Once she got inside the building, she signed her name and waited; two hours and ten minutes later, she *finally* got to see the doctor. Once the doctor came in, he told her she would need to change her medicine; as she expected, the new medicine would be more expensive. Afterwards, she called a cab to drive her home; nearly thirty minutes later, a cab arrived. On the trip home, they got stuck behind a wreck and waited for over an hour—the cab's meter running all the while. Finally, when Edith got to her apartment, she picked up her mail and discovered that she was being billed again for a bill that she had already paid. Three times she had written this company and told them that she had paid the bill. And then, to top everything, as Edith walked into her living room, she discovered that her little dog Sparky had left a *package* for her right in the middle of the living room floor. Yes, Edith has had a bad day. Or has she?

Let's think a little bit more deeply about the day Edith has experienced. Sure, she had to make a trip to the doctor. But her doctor is one of the best in the city, and truthfully, one of the best in the world. *Many people* would love to be able to go to the doctor, and they would be especially blessed to see her particular doctor. It's true that a button came off of her favorite dress, but Edith has a closet full of dresses. Many would be grateful to have more than one change of clothes. Edith was convinced that the cab driver had cheated her, but in fact, he really hadn't. You see, Edith is somewhat paranoid—and extremely money-conscious. She thinks people cheat her all the time; in fact, they have not done so. Yes, she did have to wait almost two hours to see her doctor. But during that period of time in the waiting room she was able to visit with a friend that she hadn't seen in over a year. Her doctor has changed her to new medicine, but this new medicine will work much better than what she is now taking. Yes, she sat in the cab, waiting for over an hour for the wreck to be cleared; but she wasn't *in the wreck*. And that bill that Edith had received, the bill that she had already paid was really small. Even if she had to pay it again, it would not strain her income. And as for Sparky, and his little package in the middle of the living room floor . . . Well, Sparky is her best friend in all the world. What would she do without him?

Has Edith *really* had a bad day? Or has she simply had a typically frustrating day, like we all experience from time to time? You see, it's all a matter of perspective. Is the glass half-full or half-empty? If Edith focuses her attention on the things that have gone wrong, it might be considered a bad day. On the other hand, if Edith could simply focus on the positives, her day wasn't all that difficult; it certainly could have been worse. If Edith could gain a better perspective, she could, perhaps, deliver herself from her misery, much of which she created. This isn't to say that there aren't days that can legitimately be called "bad days." Bad things do happen. The point is, however, often we make our days good or bad based on our own interpretation, our own perspective. God has given to each of us *the ability to interpret.* That's a gift that animals who inhabit this earth do not have; they are not interpreting beings. We, however, are created in the image of God. Consequently, our Creator gave us the ability to decide, to choose, to interpret. Hear the Word of the Lord: "Therefore, as God's chosen people, holy and dearly loved, clothe yourselves with compassion, kindness, humility, gentleness, and patience" (Col. 3:12). This, then, is the day that God has given you. Good things will happen; bad things will happen. The question is: "How will you interpret the experiences of this particular day?" Edith had a bad day. *Or did she?*

☺ **Smile Awhile!**

From Katy, age three, with language still a bit imprecise; "Kyle" is her brother. Miss Katy is joyfully twirling around the room on her tiptoes: "Mommy, you fwustrated with Dyle? You not fwustrated with me!"

David, Your Choice!

I have heard it said that inside of each of us is a black dog and a white dog. The one that has control is the one we feed! I know I have days when I suddenly realize that I am feeding the black dog. When that happens, I must, if it's to be a good day, make some changes inside myself. It helps to remind myself each day that I have the capacity to choose. When I feel myself living in what I call the "hurry-worry-flurry mode," I will stop what I am doing, and inject into my day a time of prayer and stillness. Ten minutes of quiet reflection can help me change the direction of my entire day–one good day at a time. The *black dog* within me might say, "You don't have time to stop and pray; you don't want your day to be slow and simple. What you want is to be driven and compulsive!" When I hear that black dog, I know that it is not the voice of the Holy Spirit, but the voice of the Evil One, who would rob me of the abundant life. And I know that the responsibility to make good choices falls directly in my lap. On one particular day, I wrote myself these words:

> *"Dear David, This day will be exactly what you choose to make it. No person, circumstance, or responsibility will get you down, except by your own choice. Today will bring evil, and today will bring good. Where will you put your focus? Today will bring fairness, and today will bring unfairness. Upon which will you shine the spotlight? Stress and anxiety will overwhelm you this day only if you allow them to do so. You can be a victim ('Poor little me! Look what life is doing to me!'); or you can be victorious, and experience the wonder, joy, and peace that God gives to His children. This day, you can*

be ego-driven, or you can be Spirit-led. David, it's your choice!"

** A HUMOROUS INTERLUDE **

A Very Good Day!

My youngest grandson is a little sweetie! He is busy—too busy for kisses that is! My little girls liked to sit on my lap and draw pictures with pawpaw. If I gave them a little kiss now and then, that was OK. But my little fellow—he's two—he likes cars with wheels, balls that bounce, trains that toot—but not kisses! Recently, when our children and grandchildren were visiting, we decided to watch a movie. My little fellow sat on the floor and played with toys. I took my five-year-old grandson on my lap to explain parts of the movie. Well—here came my two-year-old with a "car-car"; he wanted on pawpaw's lap as well! The two-year-old watched a little of the movie, and showed me his little car and its wheels. Could I sneak in a kiss or two? I did it! A kiss on a soft little cheek!

Could I do it again? Yes! A kiss on the ear and on the other cheek! Ever so gently the corners of his mouth turned upward. He was enjoying pawpaw's attention and affection. Will he let me kiss him tomorrow? Probably not! After all, there are cars with wheels, balls that bounce, and trains that toot! *But today, today! Kisses! Man, what a day*!

Jesus

Alpha and Omega

The Beginning and The End

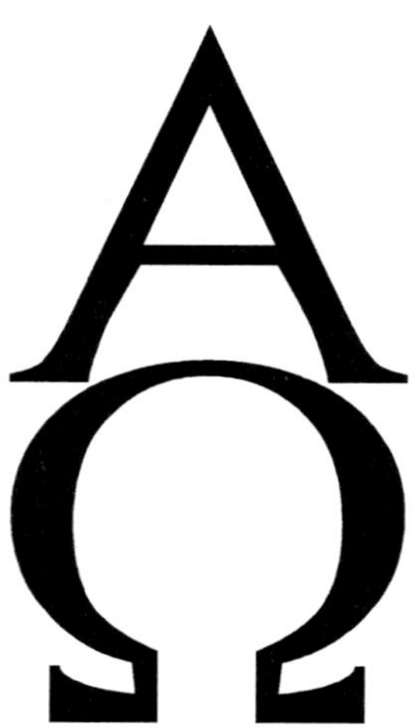

Chapter Six

Fast and Slow

Slow, Simple, and Soulful

My wife and I have a motto which we share with each other on an almost daily basis: "Darling, be sure to live today in a way that is *slow, simple and soulful*!" This is our way of reminding each other we are spiritual beings, created in God's image, and intended to live as his children. Consider the alternative to the above prescription of slow, simple, and soulful: a life that is *fast, complex and ego-driven*. Living in this manner cannot satisfy the deep spiritual needs that God has placed within us. I heard one fellow say, "There are only two groups of people in the world: 'the saints' and 'the ain'ts'!" In the New Testament, the *saints* are God's *holy* people, *set apart* by God for his glory. As Peter wrote, "But you are a chosen people, a royal priesthood, a holy nation, a people belonging to God, that you may declare the praises of him who called you out of darkness into his wonderful light" (1 Peter 2:9). Peter is reminding us: "Remember who you are!" Even better, "Remember *whose* you are!" My message in this book is simple: You and I belong to God! Let's live as his children.

How We Define Ourselves

Do you, like me, ever find yourself *driven and compulsive,* rather than living a gentle and simple life? How much can I get done today? Was I more productive today than I was yesterday? From your reading of Luke's Gospel, perhaps you recall how Martha became angry at her sister, Mary, for not helping with the preparations of the meal. Martha was blunt in her question to Jesus: "Lord, don't you care that my sister has left me to do the work by myself? Tell her to help me!" (Luke 10:40). As we read this account, we surely must have *some* sympathy for Martha. A fairly large crowd was coming to eat and the meal was not prepared. How could Mary possibly lounge at Jesus' feet with so much work to be done? Doesn't someone have to see that things get done? Of course they do! Without those people who set themselves to the task and stay with it, the world would be in sorry shape. Nevertheless, Jesus rebuked Martha: "Martha, Martha, you are worried and upset about many things, [42] but only one thing is needed. Mary has chosen what is better, and it will not be taken away from her" (Luke 10:41-42). Notice that Jesus admonishes Martha to simplify her life; that included getting her priorities straight. For Martha, *the meal had become more important than the Honored Guest*! Martha's sister Mary, on the other hand, knew how to put the First, first. Mary desired to spend time in her Lord's presence and experience his love; in him was wholeness and healing. Jesus told Martha, and he also tells us, that life doesn't have to be so difficult ("but only *one thing* is needed").

As we read this episode from Luke 10, we have to think that Jesus was not rebuking Martha for doing what needed to be done. Rather, Jesus was concerned about her inner disposition. I think Ken Gire's description of Martha is right-on: "There was no quiet center that Martha was working from, no solitude of heart, no still axis around which her activities revolved. That's why the wheels fell off her attitude" (Windows, p. 35). Martha lived to get things done—even if her approach did spiritual and psychological damage; she was trapped in a *compulsive lifestyle*. That approach to life *seems productive*; but from our Lord's perspective, it is anything but. Luke 10:40 calls Martha "distracted"; the King James version says she was "cumbered." The same word is used to describe the unproductive fig tree in Luke 13:7. One version translates as follows: "But Martha was worrying over the big dinner she was preparing" (The New Living Translation). Literally, we might say, Martha was all *twisted-up inside*; she was allowing herself to be pulled in a dozen directions—a bundle of hurry, worry, and flurry.

I don't have a bit of trouble identifying with Martha; I can easily get in that *driven-mode*. I have to remind myself daily that believers don't treat life like one *great emergency* to be solved. I love the Lord's response to Martha as reflected in the New American Standard Version: "Martha, Martha, you are worried and bothered about so many things; [42] but only a few things are necessary, really only one, for Mary has chosen the good part, which shall not be taken away from her" (Luke 10:41-42). Who knows? Perhaps these words caused Martha to examine the entire structure of her life, to ask herself, "What matters most?"

Don't many of us, like Martha, *define ourselves* by how much we achieve? I am reminded of the words which were used to describe superman in the older TV episodes: "Faster than a speeding bullet; more powerful than a locomotive; able to leap tall buildings in a single bound!" Our culture promotes this lifestyle. The result? Generations of people who are *ten miles wide and one inch deep*! I remember reading of one man whose wife asked him, "Would you be willing to be less productive in order to save our marriage?" By his actions, his answer was no. This hyper-productive approach does not make for strong marriages, families or friendships. Relationships flourish when we spend *relaxed time* with each other. That includes our relationship with the Ultimate Other—God. When I have a really busy day, it's more difficult for me to get into my prayer time. It takes about twenty to twenty-five minutes for my noisy heart to settle; then I can have a peaceful interaction with my Creator. But the busier I am, the more I need my quiet time—if I am to keep life gentle and simple.

"Simple Abundance"

Norman Cousins writes, "The clock provides only a technical measurement of how long we live. Far more real than the ticking of time is the way we open up the minutes and invest them with meaning." He continues, "Death is not the ultimate tragedy in life." As a Christian, I don't see death as a *tragedy,* rather as a *transition* into a better world. But from Cousins' perspective, what is *life's ultimate tragedy*? Is it not *to live without living at all*? That is, to simply *exist* without smelling, touching, tasting, hearing, and seeing; how unnecessary! Our hearts can be taken captive by a secular culture that clings to the false illusion of *the extraordinary*: "Life will begin when I win the lottery!" Or, "When Grandpa leaves me a large inheritance, my life can finally begin!" My friend, if you are waiting to win the lottery or for a large bequest before your life finally begins, *your life is already over*! The happiest people I have known in my lifetime have had almost nothing of what this world counts most valuable. They are not rich, famous, or powerful; but they are *content*! They have what is sometimes called "simple abundance." They appreciate those blessings that cannot be purchased: like loving relationships, deeds of kindness, or the splendors of nature. David proclaimed, "The heavens declare the glory of God; the skies proclaim the work of his hands" (Psalm 19:1). I described this "soulful" approach to life in my poem, which I entitled "All is Well."

All is Well

A gorgeous sunset splashed across the western sky;
"Oh God, help me see before I die!"

A sunlit walk without haste;
An apple freshly fallen; oh what taste!

A baby holds my finger—loves sweet embrace;
Exploding joy, this touch of grace.

I have mown spring's first grass;
Such fragrance! I must not let this moment pass.

The leaves, the bud, the rose, the thorn,
A gift this very morning born.

To see, to touch, to taste, to smell.
"Thank you God; all is well!"

☺ Smile Awhile!

I was so excited to take my five-year-old grandson, Kyle, to his first basketball game. The fact that we had to stand in line for an hour for tickets did not diminish the thrill of this occasion. Finally, we entered the large arena and found our seats. The band was playing, the cheerleaders shouting, and the teams warming up. I looked over at Kyle and noticed he had covered both ears with his hands! "What's the matter Kyle?" "*It's too loud!*" he said. I just knew that when the game started his hands would come down. Nope! The entire game his hands were up, except when he ate a snack; then, one hand stayed on an ear. With raised voice I asked, "Are you having a good time?" He shook his head affirmatively.

Slow is Best

To enjoy this *soulful* approach to life we must teach ourselves not to hurry; a quiet mind requires an unrushed life. What's the hurry anyway? Why does American culture seem to be obsessed with speed? If you drive the highways, like me you have had people pass you at twenty or thirty miles an hour over the speed limit. Even in construction zones, where men and women are working within a few feet of fast moving cars, drivers have a hard time letting-up on the gas peddle. Imagine attempting to varnish a kitchen table—while *a family is eating lunch on it*! That's what it's like for highway crews working to improve our roads; they deserve our thanks and our caution! I have had cars come up on my bumper and drive within inches, even though I am driving four or five miles an hour over the posted speed limit. Sometimes I just pull off the road, so they can get around; better that, than a bad accident. Even snow or ice doesn't slow some folks down. Believe me, that kind of driving will eventually catch up with you. The time saved on the road may be spent in the hospital or in a wheel chair—or worse. My wife and I made a declaration several years ago that we were going to drive in the slow lane; if you want to pass, be our guest. I don't mean that we drive slower than is safe, but we don't drive much over the speed limit. We prefer to be passed, rather than pass.

I like the story told by Tricia McCary Rhodes. A biologist went to an African country to study vegetation. He hired some natives to help transport equipment as they traveled afoot into the deep jungle. The first day they covered a lot of ground. He thought to himself, "Another couple of days like this, and we will reach our destination." But the next day, the natives refused to move. "Why?" asked the scientist. Through an interpreter, the natives responded: "We went too hard and fast yesterday; today we must wait for our souls to catch up to our bodies!" Our souls know when it's time to slow down, but only if we are listening!

Whatever you are doing, do it slower. Rushing turns almost every activity into a stressful event. Even pleasurable hobbies like gardening or working with flowers can be ruined by crowding too much into the available time. A wrist watch can easily be turned into a stress machine! How long does it take to eat a meal? I've seen folks wolf-down an entire meal in five to seven minutes. When we eat too quickly, we don't enjoy our food to the fullest. To be thoroughly enjoyed, food must be savored. The same is true of life itself. In very busy times, I have to *pray myself* into a slower frame of mind.

I find that sometimes I just need to be alone. When I have been *over-exposed* to people, my spirit craves solitude. It's like I can only hear the Lord if I am willing to shut out all the other voices around me. A long walk and talk with my Father will most often set things right. On occasion I will shut down in my den and listen to classical music; I find I can pray and listen at the same time. Perhaps a gentle stroll through the woods? We won't all do it the same, but each of us, I believe, needs to carve out some alone time and listen for that "small still Voice."

My favorite form of exercise is walking. For years and years I suffered from painful corns. I just assumed that foot pain was part of the price we pay for getting older. Then one day my wife said, "David, why don't you try buying shoes that are just a little wider." I was reluctant to accept her advice, because, as a boy, I had a bad experience with hand-me-down shoes that were too wide; they were miserable! Finally, however, I decided to give her suggestion a go; I bought some wider walking shoes. Within a couple of months, my corns were completely gone! *Just a little space* made all the difference in the

world. We just might be surprised to find the difference it would make, if we would give our *souls a little more space*!!

Prayer: When Life Gets Hectic

"Father, When life gets hectic, I tend to speed up. Sometimes I run ahead of you. When something inside of me cries, "Go!!" Help me say "No!" Slow is best. AMEN."

☺ **Smile Awhile!**

Two of our grandchildren found it better to retain food in their mouths, rather than to swallow it. This was especially true if they were instructed to eat something they did not like. Consider Andrew, age two. Out with his other grandparents, he ate a hamburger at Wendy's. *Three hours later*, Grandpa Wilbur saw him swallow. Andrew said: "Hamburger gone!"

<u>Life is Not a Race.</u>

A friend sent me this poem which was written by a terminally ill young girl in a New York hospital. As I understand, it was circulated by her doctor, though I do not know her name.

SLOW DANCE

"Have you ever watched kids
On a merry-go-round?

Or listened to the rain
Slapping on the ground?

“Ever followed a butterfly's erratic flight?
Or gazed at the sun into the fading night?

You better slow down.
Don't dance so fast.
Time is short.
The music won't last.

Do you run through each day
On the fly?
When you ask, “How are you?”
Do you hear the reply?

When the day is done
Do you lie in your bed
With the next hundred chores
Running through your head?

You better slow down.
Don't dance so fast.
Time is short.
The music won't last.

Ever told your child,
“We'll do it tomorrow?”
And in your haste,
Not seen his sorrow?

Ever lost touch,
Let a good friendship die
Cause you never had time
To call and say, "Hi!"

You better slow down.
Don't dance so fast.
Time is short.
The music won't last.

When you run so fast to get somewhere
You miss half the fun of getting there.
When you worry and hurry through your day,
It is like an unopened gift . . .
Thrown away.

Life is not a race.
Take it slower!
Take time to hear the music
Before the concert is over!

** A HUMOROUS INTERLUDE **

"Will playing hurt 'bounded'?"

For one period, before switching to the third grade, Mary Faith taught first grade. One day in March, the weather was nice, so Mary Faith decided to take her children outside to play. One little chubby fellow named, Joey, raised his hand. "Teacher, my mother says I am 'bounded.' Will playing outside hurt bounded?" This first grade teacher had to think a moment about *bounded*. Ah, yes, a condition sometimes treated with a laxative! Teachers know how to deal with sensitive issues: "No, Joey, playing outside will not hurt *bounded*. In fact, it might help!" The other children heard the exchange, but had no comprehension of the situation. One little girl seemed upset. "What's the matter, Christy?" With hands on hips and irritation in her voice, Christy said: "Well, when I am *grounded*, I don't get to play outside!" Just another day in the life of a teacher!

Chapter Seven

The "Old Self" and the "New Self"

The New Life

Paul tells us that when we gave our lives to Christ, we put off the "old self" and put on the "new self" (Eph. 4:24 and Col. 3:10). In Colossians the Apostle describes that process in this manner: "For you died, and your life is now hidden with Christ in God" (Col. 3:3). Paul exhorts believers to live according to the standards of this new life in Christ, for we are "created to be like God in true righteousness and holiness" (Eph. 4:24). With this new life, we no longer set our minds on "earthly things" like: "anger, rage, malice, slander, and filthy language" (Col. 3:8). Instead, our minds are focused on "things above." Paul describes believers as "God's chosen people, holy and dearly loved," clothed in "compassion, kindness, humility, gentleness and patience" (Col. 3:12).

I like to make a distinction between what I call "mosquitoes" and "malaria." Malaria, of course can kill you; it's potentially very dangerous. Mosquitoes, on the other hand, are almost always just irritating. They bite, cause an itch, and are gone. But I continually see people who confuse *mosquitoes* with *malaria*. That is, they take little things that don't amount to a hill of

beans and blow them up into humongous problems. Think of the stress that causes! In truth, most of our troubles are solved by ignoring them! I have said to others and also to myself, "Remember, friend, this is just a mosquito, not malaria. Give it a day or two, and it will be gone!"

Do you see it? People who live day after day in anger, rage, malice, slander, and bitterness are just miserable! They live in a battle zone; life is *a war they have to win*. On the other hand, folks clothed with "compassion, kindness, humility, gentleness, and patience" live in a different Kingdom! Life for them is doxology. Their only decision is, "Who do I, in the name of Christ, love next?" Can you think of a better way to *simplify your life*? I understand the gravitational pull of the old self, the sinful nature. I know that people can say and do the most inconsiderate things. Most often: ignore it! Also, don't forget that we do not fight this battle alone; the Holy Spirit lives in us! We need not be controlled by our sinful natures. Hear the Word of the Lord: "If by the Spirit you put to death the misdeeds of the body, you will live, [14] because those who are led by the Spirit of God are sons of God" (Romans 8:13-14). We are not *driven* by our old natures but *led* by God's Spirit! We don't live in that old house anymore!

My New Residence

(DAE)

I moved into a new house today;
With God's help, I'm here to stay.

My new residence is a House of Love;
A gift from God above.

My dwelling place is not too big or too small;
Inside there is room for all.

My residence is not too hot or too cold,
And it will never grow old.

I don't care if it's day or night;
My new place is just right.

As long as I live in this house, I'll never be alone;
I'll always have God's Spirit as my very own!

In this place, Jesus is near;
In his presence, I have nothing to fear!

In my house, which is completely new,
My God, there will always be a room reserved for You!

** A HUMOROUS INTERLUDE **

I dropped him!

I ministered for seven and one-half years in Indianapolis, Indiana. We had a young man who had surrendered his life to the Lord, and he was ready to be baptized. Well, I thought, why not start Easter service with a baptism? There was one problem; the man was tall—as in six-feet-five. I am five-feet-ten! I said to this good gentleman, "It will be imperative that you bend your knees as I immerse you, or I will not be able to support your weight." The church building was packed that Easter morning, and I was excited to begin with a baptism. But we experienced one *big* problem: the fellow forgot to bend his knees. About half way down, I knew I could not continue to support his weight. I had to drop him, or we were both going under! When I let go, water splashed out of the baptistry; and the congregation struggled to restrain its laughter. I said to this young man: "You will never forget your baptism!" I haven't forgotten it either!

The New Self and the Old Life

I am truly grateful for the "new self" that God has given me. To have the Holy Spirit, God's Comforter and Counselor, living in me is wonderful. I love "my new house" and would not want to live anywhere else. *However*! I still have days when I lose perspective. When I'm exhausted and over-extended, I can transform life from a celebration to a David-centered pity-party. Often I am embarrassed to look back at my journal entries and see how difficult I made life on a particular day. Sometimes I am amazed at my capacity to make life *anything but simple and gentle*—as in the following entry from my journal.

**

"Something is wrong; very wrong! I feel stressed, over-worked, overwhelmed; burnout crouches at the door of my life. Just a few weeks ago I was telling Mary Faith, "I have never been more filled with the joy of the Lord. This is the best time of my life." Where did that joy, peace, and contentment go? If we had a dark, musty basement that leaked water, I would plop myself down in the darkest corner and eat mud pies. I cry out day and night against the injustices of life. I know exactly how Job felt; I am in a funk! Life has been so unfair to me.

- *"It's been raining for days. Doesn't the Lord know I need a little sunshine?*
- *"My car has a mechanical problem that comes and goes; it comes when I am driving it and goes when I try to show it to the mechanic.*
- *"I spent hours working on a lecture for one of the college classes I teach; such* pearls of wisdom *I gave my students. After the lecture one student said, "I didn't understand a word you said!"*
- *"The dentist says I have a cracked tooth that is going to require an expensive crown; joy, joy, joy!*
- *"I said, 'Yes,' to writing a book review for a scholarly journal, but I don't have time to read the book, or write the review!*

- *"This morning when I tried to open the cereal box, the lid tore into a dozen pieces. When I attempted to pull apart the plastic bag inside, it would not give. I am fairly strong, but the bag was unyielding. I was ready to take it downstairs to my band saw, when it broke loose and spilled cereal all over the kitchen!*

"Something is wrong! Life is doing me dirty; I just feel like a giant kitty litter box and the world is dumping on me!"

**

I'm reminded of a statement from one of the characters in the Mitford Series by Jan Karon. Percy, having a bad day, says, "All I lack of bein' dead is th' news getting out." Have you ever felt this way? If not, perhaps you should be writing this book! I don't have a lot of days like that, but I have some. What's wrong? Well, on that occasion I was exhausted, burned out; I was neglecting my quiet time with the Lord, and trying to be *too productive*. I had taken on too many responsibilities. If only I had been willing to say, "No, I can't do that; I am already too busy." Honestly, I was living, not as a child of God, but as a pagan—as *a man of the ego* and not *a person of the soul*. In my quiet time, I could hear Jesus say to me: "[David, David,] you are worried and upset about many things, [42] but only one thing is needed" (Luke 10:41-42).

Prayer: Burned Out!

"Lord, I feel burned out; I am focusing on all the wrong things. Help me not to regret, over expect, make mountains out of molehills. I'm feeling like a victim—under-appreciated and overworked. Yet Lord, by your great power, help me recover my perspective and get beyond my dark mood. Give me rest for my tired soul. Lord, I don't know anyone more blessed than me. I am saved by your grace and filled with your Spirit. O God, that is more than enough! Help me to know what I already know. Thank you, Father, for understanding. I accept your gift of wholeness and healing. In Jesus' Name. AMEN."

☺ Smile Awhile!

Allison, age two: Allison was visiting her aunt and uncle's new apartment for the first time. She wanted some juice, so Aunt Christy handed her a box of apple juice. Mawmaw, concerned about possible spills on the carpet, said, "Don't squeeze." Allison sipped some juice and stood staring at the box with its straw. She said, "I no squeeze. I no squeeze." Then, with a mischievous look, she said, "I squeezed!!"

Chapter Eight

Rich and Poor

Our culture tries to tell us that if we really want to live happy, fulfilled lives, then we must live to please ourselves. We need to accumulate all the money that we can possibly get—all the power, all the achievement, all the sex—these are the things that matter in an *ego-driven culture*. Solomon tried that way of life, as is reflected in Ecclesiastes. Hear his words, "I denied myself nothing my eyes desired. I refused my heart no pleasure. My heart took delight in all my work, and this was the reward for all my labor. Yet, when I surveyed all that my hands had done and what I had toiled to achieve, everything was meaningless, a chasing after the wind" (2:10-11). As Solomon discovered, true happiness cannot be found in the empty pleasures that this world offers. Jesus put the question succinctly: "What good will it be for a man if he gains the whole world, yet forfeits his soul? Or what will a man give in exchange for his soul?" (Matt. 16:26).

☺ **Smile Awhile!**

Mr Kyle in a prayer he said when age four: "Dear Jesus, Thank you for everything we do. Thank you for everything we need. Thank you for Corvettes. But we know we don't get everything when we go to the store. But I need a corvette. Amen."

The Upside-Down Kingdom!

What if the world were upside-down? What if you went up to mow the grass, and down to fly a kite? What if sand was as valuable as diamonds, and diamonds were worthless? What if horses could fly and bite, and we could ride mosquitoes? Silly? Surely! And intended to make a point. My friend, if you are a Christian, *you and I are part of an Upside- Down Kingdom.* To follow the example of Jesus is to follow the path the saints have trod throughout the generations. To live in this Upside-Down Kingdom may mean facing the wrath of our secular world. Through the generations, many believers have surrendered *their very lives* in order to walk in His footsteps. Jesus was the most loving man who ever lived; but he was also the most hated! Jesus warned us that "All men will hate you because of me, but he who stands firm to the end will be saved" (Matt.

10:22). Is it any wonder that in his kingdom we have to become "nothing" from this world's perspective, in order to become "something" from God's perspective? Think about God's kingdom, and remember that it's an Upside-Down Kingdom! Consider:

- Our King was born in a manger; His throne was a cross.
- To save your life is to lose it; to lose your life is to find it.
- The first will be last, and the last will be first.
- To serve is more honorable than to be served.
- If we exalt ourselves, we will be humbled; if we humble ourselves, we will be exalted.
- The rich in this kingdom are often poor in spirit.
- The meek will inherit the earth.
- It is more blessed to give than to receive.
- We are called to love our enemies, and pray for those who would hurt or offend us.
- In order to live, we must die.
- In our weakness, we find his strength.
- Our eyes are focused not on what is seen, but on what is not seen.

Prayer: Building Your Kingdom

"Lord, for me the switch seems to happen so easily. One moment I am a humble servant working in the background to achieve your purposes in the world. Then suddenly I find myself in a different universe; one in which I am the sun, the moon, and the stars! I find myself obsessed with what other people think about me. Am I perceived as a success? Father, I repent of my selfishness, and offer myself to achieve your glory. I want to play a part in the building of your Upside-Down Kingdom; I know this kingdom can have only One who is Lord. AMEN."

The Rich Young Ruler

In Luke 18:18-30, we have a wealthy young man, who came to Jesus asking, "Good teacher, what must I do to inherit eternal life?" (Luke 18:18). The context of this passage makes it apparent that this rich young ruler was basically a good man. For the most part, he had kept the Ten Commandments. Yet, this wealthy man had made one giant mistake; he defined himself by his worldly goods. God was on his list, but not at the top of his list. He would follow Jesus, but only if he could keep his money and possessions *at the top.* Realizing this, Jesus said to him, "You still lack one thing. Sell everything you have, and give to the poor, and you will have treasure in heaven. Then come, and follow me" (Luke 18:22). The words of our Lord went directly into this young man's heart. And perhaps for a few fleeting seconds he considered forsaking his riches and following the

Master. But, alas, he could not do so. From his perspective, if he gave away his money, he would be "nothing." Exactly! That's why Jesus said: "How hard it is for the rich to enter the kingdom of God" (Luke 18:24).

Does this mean that in order to follow Jesus every faithful believer must give away all of his or her possessions to the poor? Not necessarily. I believe Jesus is saying: "Put Me first! If anything on your list comes ahead of me, then you must be willing to surrender it!" Some people think it's possible to follow in the footsteps of Jesus and still keep their money or their possessions *at the top of the list*. Our Lord made it clear that this is not the case. Jesus said: "For where your treasure is, there your heart will be also" (Matt. 6:21). Remember, if we want to be a part of the Upside-Down Kingdom, we must follow the dictates of the King! Once we do so, *life gets easier*! Listen to Jesus: "Take my yoke upon you and learn from me, for I am gentle and humble in heart, and you will find rest for your souls. [30] For my yoke is easy and my burden is light" (Matt. 11:29-30). How can we take upon ourselves *a yoke*; and yet, have life get *easier*? How is his burden light? It's simple: *Jesus helps us pull the load!*

<u>Cash in the Trash</u>?

Let's imagine a scene like this: a garbage man comes to pick up someone's trash. The trash collector is shocked to see that in the trash can there are all kinds of valuable objects, including money. The collector sees furs, diamonds, pearls, even hundred dollar bills in the trash can. Being honest, the man is convinced that he cannot simply appropriate these riches to himself. He sees the owner of the property working in his yard. "Sir, I wonder if you realize what's in your trash can?" *"Oh yes, I know what's in my trash can."* "But sir, it's full of furs, diamonds, pearls, even cash! There is cash in your trash!" The owner replies: *"My wife and I purposefully decided to throw all of those objects in the trash can, including the cash! You see, we have recently become Christians. And one night we sat down and had a long talk. We decided that if we didn't get rid of some things, we were going to be tempted to revert to our old life. Don't worry; we kept enough to live on. We don't want the rest; it's yours. But I warn you, be careful. That stuff is downright dangerous!"*

☺ **Smile Awhile!**

A man once stood up in the back of a public bus and said loudly, "Has anyone on the bus lost a large sum of money with a rubber band tied around it?" Immediately six hands went into the air. Responded the man, "Well, I just wanted you to know I found the rubber band!"

To Know Christ

It's interesting to see the transformation that came over Paul's life once he became a Christian. Before his conversion, Paul lived for himself. He spent his energies promoting his own agenda, building his own kingdom of "legalistic righteousness!" After his conversion, he lived for God and for others. Before his conversion, the Apostle Paul was a man who put his trust, not in God, but in himself; his confidence was "in the flesh." Paul tells the Philippians that before his conversion, he had every reason to put confidence in the flesh. Listen as he describes his pre-Christian life: "If anyone else thinks he has reason to put confidence in the flesh, I have more: circumcised on the eighth day, of the people of Israel, of the tribe of Benjamin; a Hebrew of Hebrews; in regard to the law, a Pharisee; as for zeal, persecuting the church; as for legalistic righteousness, faultless" (Philip. 3:4-6). Paul indicates that before his conversion, *he really did not need God*. You see, in a sense, he was saving himself with all of his "spiritual achievements." Prior to his conversion to the Christian faith, his life centered on legalistic acts of righteousness. But, on the road to Damascus, Saul (Paul) encountered the living Christ; his life was radically transformed.

Listen to Paul as he defines his life *after* becoming a Christian: "But whatever was to my profit, I now consider loss for the sake of Christ. What is more, I consider everything a loss compared to the surpassing greatness of knowing Christ Jesus my

Lord, for whose sake I have lost all things. I consider them rubbish, that I may gain Christ . . . " (Philip. 3:7-8). Says Paul, when I gave my life to Jesus Christ, I realized that all of those human things that I put my confidence in no longer mattered: my credentials, the fact that I belong to the right family, my circumcision, my legalistic righteousness. Paul turned his back on all these when he became a part of the Upside-Down Kingdom!

I like to say it like this: after surrendering his life to Christ, *Paul put his cash in the trash*. He no longer felt the need to prove himself. He wasn't living any longer "after the flesh," but "after the Spirit." He became a man of the *soul,* rather than the *ego*: "I want to know Christ and the power of His resurrection, and the fellowship of sharing in his sufferings, becoming like him in his death, and so somehow to attain the resurrection from the dead" (Philip. 3:10ff). All of the things that were important to him *before* Christ, no longer mattered.

The heretics who tried to get the Philippians to live by the law (by the *ego*!) were called, by Paul in Philippians 2, "dogs" or "mutilators of the flesh" (Philip. 3:2). These agitators were not leading the Philippians to a more dedicated life, or even to a happier life. They were leading them *away* from God and *away* from the abundant life. These false teachers were saying: "You don't need God; you can do it yourself!" Paul told the Philippians, "Watch out for those dogs . . . !" Beware of the dogs; beware of those people who try to tell you that life is found in the ego and not in the soul. Remember, my friends: "Beware of dogs!"

What say ye? What is your "cash"? Are you sufficiently desirous of a gentle and simple life to put your "cash in the trash"? Is it your supreme passion that you might "know Christ and the power of His resurrection, and the fellowship of sharing in his sufferings"?

** A HUMOROUS INTERLUDE **

"Beware of Dog!"

I once visited a children's home in Virginia. The children who lived in this home had a large pet, which they shared. The dog was a Saint Bernard, and it appeared to be as tame as any dog I have ever seen. In fact, the children would actually ride this Saint Bernard. Imagine my shock when one day, as I was leaving the cafeteria, this dog decided I was his mortal enemy. He was lying by the door and appeared to be asleep. He opened one eye, looked at me, walked over slowly, got a hold of my leg with his teeth, and chewed violently for three or four seconds. Then he let go, went back over, and lay down. It won't surprise you that since that time, I have had a healthy respect for dogs—especially large Saint Bernards!

☺ **Smile Awhile!**

Mr Kyle, age two: Kyle was enamored with animals, but didn't have them all sorted out yet. He was going to the golf course with Grandpa, when he saw a brown cow in a field. His response: "Whoa! Big dog!"

Spiritual Wealth

With respect to spiritual wealth, do you know that God considers believers to be *rich*? A gentle and simple life requires that we keep our eyes forever fixed on Jesus, the one who made himself "nothing." The Apostle Paul described Jesus in this manner: "For you know the grace of our Lord Jesus Christ, that though he was rich, yet for your sakes he became poor, so that you through his poverty might become rich" (2 Cor. 8:9). On one occasion Jesus said to his disciples, "Blessed are you who are poor, for yours is the kingdom of God" (Luke 6:20). Once, in describing all of the hardships he encountered in ministry, Paul described himself as "sorrowful, yet always rejoicing; poor, yet making many rich; having nothing, and yet possessing everything" (2 Cor. 6:10). Note that for Paul, *material prosperity* was not necessary in order to "possess everything."

If Christ Jesus is our Lord, *we are rich*! From a spiritual perspective, then, the question is not, "Are we rich?" But rather: "Do we *acknowledge* that we are rich and are we *thankful*?" The Apostle Paul desperately wanted believers to acknowledge and appreciate the gift of God's grace as revealed in Christ Jesus: "I pray also that the eyes of your heart may be enlightened in order that you may know the hope to which he has called you, the riches of his glorious inheritance in the saints, [19] and his incomparably great power for us who believe" (Eph. 1:18-19). Paul could not think of enough ways to thank God for his grace revealed in the life, death, and resurrection of Jesus.

I can't think of a better time for us to express our appreciation to God for his Gift *than right now.*

☺ Smile Awhile!

Andrew, age two: "I'm a 'choo-choo-train-doggie-car.' I say, 'Choo, choo; vroom, vroom; and woof, woof!'"

Chapter Nine

"If" and "Is"!

Have you known people who always dwell in *the winter of discontent*? They just cannot seem to find "it"— whatever "it" may be. But what is *it*? Perhaps a change of jobs will be the answer, or even a new wife! One day they want a larger bank account, the next day a larger house, and the next a fancier car. John D. Rockefeller was once asked, "How much money does it take to make a person happy?" His response, "*Just a little more*!" So it is with those who spend their energies pursuing the treasures of an earthly kingdom; their obsession with *something* prevents them from experiencing gentle and simple lives. Their houses, cars, and bank accounts may be big, but their spirituality is often *shallow*, and their souls *small*. What they truly need is a closer connection to God, but they don't realize it, or won't acknowledge it. That empty spot they feel on the inside comes from neglecting their spiritual needs. Augustine's much quoted dictum comes to mind: "You [God] have made us for yourself, and our hearts find no rest until they rest in You." Jesus said it in this manner, "Now this is eternal life, that they may know you, the only true God, and Jesus Christ, whom you have sent" (John 17:3).

How easily deceived we humans are. I sometimes express that deception as a three-pronged fork:

- *The illusion of knowing.* In truth, what seems accurate is inaccurate.
- *The delusion of self-sufficiency.* "Why do I need the Lord? I am doing quite well on my own."
- *The confusion of crossed purposes.* On the surface, we declare ourselves in service to God; in reality, we are working on our own agenda.

From a human perspective, there's always another mountain to climb, another peak to conquer. Always running, working, doing, learning, practicing, achieving, moving, climbing, buying, pushing, thinking. Yet, the pinnacle is never reached. On the inside, *mountain climbers* will always be haunted by loneliness and dissatisfaction—their deepest need, as reflected in Scripture, never met: "Be still, and know that I *am* God; I will be exalted among the nations, I will be exalted in the earth" (Psalm 46:10). I am reminded of Steven Covey's metaphor of the man who claws his way to the top of the tallest tree in the forest. As he looks around from his exalted perch, he discovers that he's *in the wrong forest*. Jesus said, "What kind of deal is it to get everything you want but lose yourself?" (Matt. 16:26; Msg.).

I Wish We'd Had Rice

I make $100,000 a year; I wish I made more!

I'm six-feet-two; I wish I were six-four!

I drive a new truck; but if I had four-wheel drive, I'd never get stuck!

I have a gun; I wish I had a knife.

I married a wonderful woman; I wish I had another wife.

Our new house is great, but a bigger one would be nice.

We had potatoes for dinner; I wish we'd had rice.

 **Smile Awhile!**

Allison at age two while assembling a three-part puzzle: "I do *everything* in the *whole world*!"

The "Unusual Tourist"

It was a small town with very few tourists. It didn't take much in this village to create news, which made its way quickly from house to house. One day *he* came; he would only say that he had a wall to build. When asked, "What wall," he simply would not answer. Instead, he worked from dawn to dusk, piling brick upon brick. Because they did not know his name, the town folk just called him "Builder." As time passed, people came to watch Builder work, and they would leave curious. The wall had no discernable pattern; it wasn't a building, just a wall connected to nothing. "What in the world is this guy doing?" No one knew but the Builder; was he deranged? As time passed, the man became more and more agitated, as if some great calamity were about to befall him. The wall was ten feet long, eight feet high, and three feet thick. As the Builder approached the completion of his project, he worked frantically. Still, he would explain his actions to no one. The day the last brick was laid, the whole town came out to see if anything happened; they were not disappointed. The Builder seemed absolutely beside himself as he dropped the last brick into place. Then, he did the strangest thing anyone from the village could remember. He carefully stepped off twenty-five paces from the wall. Then he turned, looked at the wall, lowered his head, and ran full speed, head-first into the wall! Several people rushed to his rescue, but the man was angry: "Leave me alone!" He would allow no one to help him. "Why are you doing this?" some cried. The Builder gave no response except to say, "It must be!" Over and over again, he pummeled himself against the wall; until he passed out from the pounding.

Have you known anyone like the Builder? I have known several. These people slam themselves into a wall called "reality." They find immovable objects, and spend a lifetime ramming their heads into them! For some reason, they seem to take pleasure in punishing themselves. As minister, counselor, or friend, you may cry out: "Stop! Why are you treating yourself this way? Don't you realize that you will never win this battle? Give it up!" But words often don't help; these "builders" feel some inner compulsion to harm themselves, and they won't be deterred.

This chapter I entitled "If" and "Is." I did so thinking about all those people I have known over the years who never seem to get beyond what I call the "If questions." Questions like these:

- *What if I had been born to a different family?*
- *What if I had married a different man or woman?*
- *What if I were rich?*
- *What if I had been a better athlete?*
- *What if my daughter had not gotten pregnant?*
- *What if I could change his or her personality?*
- *What if I did not have heart disease?*

"If people" worry themselves sick over things that cannot be changed. Perhaps they are some of the same kinds of people Jesus was talking about when he said, "Who of you by worrying can add a single hour to his life?" (Matt. 6:27). May I paraphrase our Lord: "Why do you keep running into that brick wall? Can't you see that it is not going to move?" "If" people often get caught in an endless cycle of discouragement and depression. They know that bumping into reality hurts, yet accepting reality seems out of the question. Let's think about it a minute: *If you cannot have what you want, what must you do?* Of course! *Learn to want what you have*. The Buddhists say, "Want what life wants." But I am not a Buddhist; I am a Christian! Christ Jesus helps me to accept what I cannot change. I am not saying that such acceptance is *easy*, but I know it's *necessary* to live a gentle and simple life. Unless we learn to accept "Is," we will never experience true contentment. Listen to the Apostle Paul:

> "I have learned to be content whatever the circumstances. [12] I know what it is to be in need, and I know what it is to have plenty. I have learned the secret of being content in any and every situation, whether well fed or hungry, whether living in plenty or in want" (Philip. 4:11-12).

How did Paul learn to be content in any and every circumstance? He tells us: "I can do everything through him who gives me strength" (Philip. 4:13). Robert Greene says it so beautifully in his poem entitled "A Mind Content."

Sweet are the thoughts that savor of content,
The quiet mind is richer than a crown—
A mind content, both crown and kingdom is.

I don't play the "If" game much any more. As I get older, I don't greatly enjoy running into brick walls! In truth, I never did really care for it, but I did it anyway—and still do sometimes! One night in devotions I wrote a poem to myself, and entitled it "Is!" It's a short poem, not strong enough to knock down brick walls, but wise enough to teach us to *walk around them*—with His help, of course!

IS!
(DAE)

If!
If only!

IS!

Should be!
Could be!

IS!

Might be!
May be!

IS!

Perhaps?
Possibly?

IS!

Life IS!
If we are HIS, IS!

A Husband With a Sharp Tongue

Once, after presenting a workshop, I had a lady come to me with tears in her eyes. I asked her the problem. She said, "My husband says some of the most cruel and hurtful things to me." She asked, "What can I ever do to change him?" As we talked, she explained that most of the time she felt her marriage was good. Her husband loved her, and most often treated her with kindness and respect. Yet, when he lost his temper, he would say some mean-spirited things. Her question: "How can I change him?" She said it wasn't fair that she should have to put up with his angry outbursts. I asked her, "How long have you been married?" She replied, "forty-eight years." "Have you been trying," I asked, "for forty-eight years to change your husband?" "Yes, I've worked at it all of those years, and yet, he does not change!" "Is it possible," I responded, "that you are going to have to learn to change yourself?" She was incredulous: "What do you mean?" "Is it possible that you are simply going to have to learn to deal with these angry outbursts by your husband? I am not saying that these are right, nor am I saying that they will ever be easy to endure. But, into every person's life there comes some unfairness." Oh, did she have trouble with my suggestion! "But it isn't right; it's not fair. *He* should be the one to change!" "My dear lady, what if he won't change? After half a century, I think that would be an accurate conclusion! Would you prefer that your husband were deceased?" "Oh no!" she said. "We love each other deeply; I would not want him to die!" "Would you prefer that either you or your husband be dealing with some catastrophic illness?" "Oh, no!" she said. "I'm very thankful that we have basically good health." "Would you prefer," I asked, "that you live in poverty, or that you had a terribly rebellious child?" Again, of course, her answer was "No!"

Soon, the lady realized the point I was making. If unfairness comes to the life of every single individual—and it does—should we not be grateful that the unfairness we face is not worse? Remember, every single one of us faces unfairness. That's the nature of life. That's the nature of the world in which we live. Just remember to give thanks for all the good things that you have in your life.

Life is Not Fair!

Please don't forget: *Life is not fair*! In this fallen world, everything that happens is not just or fair; that's the way it is. Some people are born handsome or pretty; others are not. Some have excellent health; not so of others. As a boy, I was deeply frustrated that so many others seemed to have more athletic ability than I did. The day I was cut from the basketball team, my heart was broken; I remember feeling a little angry at God. Instead of being five-feet-ten and somewhat squatty, I should have been six-feet-six and built like a rock! In the passing of years, I have discovered that, while some people have more athletic ability than me, *others have less*. Nevertheless, I've taught some fairly athletic fellows not to mess with me on the golf course!

If we are not satisfied with the person God has created us to be, life becomes too complicated. Please understand that I am not talking about accepting moral or ethical sins from which we need to repent. I am talking about our appearance, our gifts, our personality. Questions like these only make us discouraged and unhappy: "Why did God give him such confidence in social settings, while I am painfully shy and introverted?" Recall my prayer from an earlier chapter: "Lord, I thank you for the person you have made me, and for the person you are making me."

I have always enjoyed Thomas Merton's little essay on "trees." "A tree gives glory to God first by being a tree. For in being what God means it to be, it is imitating an idea which is in God and which is not distinct from the essence of God, and therefore a tree imitates God by being a tree. The more a tree is like itself, the more it is like Him. If it tried to be something else which it was never intended to be, it would be less like God and therefore it would give him less glory. . . . Therefore, each particular being, in its own characteristics, and its own private qualities . . . gives glory to God by being precisely what he wants it to be here and now, in the circumstances ordained for it by his love and infinite art."

☺ Smile Awhile!

Adrian, at age two: "I like me! Do you like you?"

Every single one of us has experienced things which we might consider unfair. But how miserable to make one's self into a victim: "Nobody treats me right, not even God!" If we are to get on with life, we must get over "it"—whatever *it* might be. I've heard it said that if all the problems of the world were put in a great pile and then divided so that each person carried exactly the same number of problems, most of us *would be grateful for the burdens we now carry*! If we wish to live simple and gentle lives, we must refuse, every day, the slippery slide into the "victim-mode." That includes some days when *we are true victims*. When that happens, we should say, "She really insulted me. I wonder what lesson God wants me to learn from this experience? Maybe he wants me to learn to forgive the way he has forgiven me." My friend, *don't get even; get smart!*

Life, you see, is about growing as a person and a Christian. It's about learning to trust God more and being satisfied with the all-sufficiency of his grace: "My grace is sufficient for you, for my power is made perfect in weakness" (2 Cor. 12:9). That's why the Apostle Paul wrote: "Therefore I will boast all the more gladly about my weaknesses, so that Christ's power may rest on me. [10] That is why, for Christ's sake, I delight in weaknesses, in insults, in hardships, in persecutions, in difficulties. For when I am weak, then I am strong" (2 Cor. 12:9-10). In a struggle with these very issues, I wrote "God's Peace Within."

God's Peace Within

With the rose, comes the thorn.
With the rainbow, comes the storm.
In the worst, we find the best.
In our heartache, we find His rest.
Love and grace,
Guilt and sin.
In good and bad,
His peace reigns within.

Prayer: Through Eyes of Grace

"My Heavenly Father, I never cease to be amazed at your grace. That you could love and forgive me is wonderful beyond words. Perhaps, Father, I could internalize that grace if I could share it with others. What he said was hurtful and cruel. Give me strength in the name of Jesus to forgive. What she did was mean-spirited and unkind; in Christ's name, I forgive her. Help me, Lord, to see people through eyes of grace, that the world might be a better place. AMEN."

** A HUMOROUS INTERLUDE **

A Swedish Proverb: *"Be true to your teeth, or your teeth will be false to you!"*

My dentist, Dr. Keys, is a fine Christian man with a very colorful personality. He often sings while he works on my teeth; at first, this unnerved me. His favorite songs are by pop artists of the 1950's, like Frank Sinatra or Dean Martin. But the first song I heard him sing was: "IT'S GOT TO BE IN THE MOLAR! IT'S GOT TO BE IN THE MOLAR!" He was correct; I had a small crack in a molar.

Recently, Dr. Keys was doing some cosmetic dental work for me. By mistake he put on more adhesive than he had planned. Quickly he said, "Well, that was a *licentious* thing to do!" In a couple of minutes he commented, "I wonder where that word came from? I don't even know what it means!" I assisted him by telling him that *"licentious"* was a biblical word that refers to excessive sinning, usually *of the sensual kind.* A little embarrassed, he said: "Well, at least it proves I have spent some time in church pews!"

Chapter Ten

Fear and Faith

The World After September 11, 2001

What does the future hold? What will tomorrow bring? If you watch the news, you know that we live in uncertain times. The world after September 11, 2001 is filled with such words as: terrorists; war; smallpox; dirty bombs; weapons of mass destruction. A kind of residual fear has planted itself in the psyche of us all. We feel vulnerable and uncertain, as we face the future. Yet, our faith in the living God should give us the strength to confront our fears. The Apostle Paul wrote: "For God hath not given us the spirit of fear; but of power, and of love, and of a sound mind" (2 Tim. 1:7; KJV). The same power that raised our Lord Jesus Christ from the dead is available to each of us!

To live one's life in fear and anxiety is to spend life in a self-inflicted cage. Victor Canning, in his novel *Birds of a Feather*, describes one of his characters, Lady Swale, in this manner:

> She was lost because she had no true spirit and no courage which sprang from deep self-respect. She lived in a cage and the unmoving conviction was full grown in her that even if one day the cage door were left open then she would still rest the victim of her deep timidity and would stay within the gilded bars of her comfortable prison.

Apparently Lady Swale would not leave her protective cage, even if the door were left open. In truth, each of us has in our hand the key that will let us out of our cage—if we truly want out. *That key is the choosing of faith over fear.*

Chased By a Tiger!

Let me illustrate our battle with fear with a simple parable.

I increased in pace as I realized that someone (or something) was following me. I could hear heavy breathing; a strange shadow flickered behind me. As I came to a street light, I quickly glanced back, and saw a huge tiger racing toward me. I broke into a full-speed run, but the animal was quicker. My lungs burned; I could not last much longer. I darted down an alley thinking that I might find safety in some unlocked door. The beast followed, his hot breath at my back. I scrambled for the only door available; the doorknob refused to turn! Fear overwhelmed me; in moments sharp teeth and claws would shred my body! I ran to the darkest corner of the alley, and in my horror, saw the beast moving in for the kill.

Unexpectedly, I felt a wave of courage surface from some deep recess of my soul. I

thought, "If I must die, I will not surrender without a fight." Not believing my own actions, I jumped at the beast, even as he lunged for me. I grabbed him by the ears, and for a split-second our eyes met in a cold stare. The tiger seemed startled at my aggressive response. With every ounce of strength within me, I shook the beast till his teeth literally rattled. I marveled at what happened next: the animal turned and ran in the opposite direction, the speed of his departure faster than when chasing me.

I know this tiger may someday return with that blood-thirsty look in his eye. If, and when he does, I may at first react with great fear. But I know that deep inside me is a rock-hard courage! You see, I now know that the animal takes flight in the face of a forthright challenge.

Have you ever been chased by a tiger? If not, your day will surely come! In fact, in life we confront one tiger after another: health problems, loss of loved ones, automobile accidents, natural disasters, terrorist threats. Amelia Earhart was correct when she wrote, "Courage is the price that life exacts for granting peace. The soul that knows it not; knows no release. . . ." Spiritual and emotional health demand that we be courageous. Either we take the tiger by the ears and shake him till his teeth rattle, or we allow him to eat us alive!

I Am Through Running!

Every believer who wants to rise above his or her fears must grow into a *faith-shaped courage*. We learn such courage as we *practice* our faith. In the face of every challenge, we choose *fear* or *faith*. Think of faith as the top of a step ladder. Each rung on the ladder represents some object, person, or situation which you fear. Every time you face your fears with determination, you move one step closer to conquering them. Viewed from this perspective, fears actually have the potential to lead us, step by step, toward a life of trust. But remember, this is an ongoing battle; we will continue to be tempted to run. Time and time again *we must choose courage over fear,* until it becomes a habit, a way of life. Our first impulse screams: "Run from the tiger!" That's the time to stop, our hand in God's. Then we grab the tiger by the ears and shake him till his teeth rattle! Easy? No! Effective? Yes!

Life on the run is no fun; it keeps us spiritually and emotionally exhausted. It's the very antithesis of a gentle and simple life. In point of fact, running makes matters worse, not better. William James wrote: "We do not run because we are afraid; we are afraid because we run." If we desire the abundant life, each of us must say, "I've had enough; I'm through running!"

"Courage" for the Believer

Does the word "courage" have a different meaning for the Christian than for the non-Christian? I answer this question with a resounding, "Yes!" When the non-Christian is courageous, he relies wholly on his own resources; he pulls himself up by his own bootstraps. The Christian also makes use of his inner strength, but he does so with the assistance of ". . . him who is able to do immeasurably more than all we ask or imagine, according to his power that is at work within us" (Eph. 3:20).

Through the years, Philippians 4:13 has given me confidence: "I can do all things through Christ which strengthens me" (KJV). That is quite different than saying, "I can do all things." In my early years of preaching and teaching, I suffered severely from stage fright. I would often repeat Philippians 4:13 to myself before preaching or teaching a lesson. The Lord is always with us when we face our tigers—regardless of what or who they might be. I also find strength in the words which God spoke to Joshua: "Have I not commanded you? Be strong and courageous. Do not be terrified; do not be discouraged, for the Lord your God will be with you wherever you go" (Josh. 1:9). Think about it; in everything we do, *our Father is there to support us*. It's not enough to simply believe in God. We must cultivate, deep within, the unmistakable conviction that He is our Ever-Present Companion. I believe Jesus spoke these words not just for the disciples, but also for us: "I will not leave you as orphans; I will come to you" (John 14:18).

You are not Alone!
(DAE)

When the heat of day would melt you …
When the cold of night would freeze you …

You are not Alone!

When the driving rains would flood you …
When the chilling winds would cut you …

You are not Alone!

When the storms of life get to you …
When the hurricanes blow through you …

You are not Alone!
You are not Alone!

☺ **Smile Awhile!**

Katy, age two: Katy has a Big Bird blanket, she calls her "Lubby" (for Lovey). One day Katy said, "When I have a storm in my window, I put 'lubby' over my head."

Faith is the Heart of Courage

How do we overcome obstacles that seem greater than us? How do we deal with inadequacy and insecurity, and learn to tackle life in a triumphant manner? How do we face a future filled with uncertainty, yet continue to live with confidence and hope? Paul asserts, "We live by faith, not by sight" (2 Cor. 5:7). Also, let us not forget the relationship between "faith" and "courage." For the Christian, *faith is the heart of courage*; faith makes courage possible. John Greenleaf Whittier wrote a dynamic poem entitled "The Rock Beneath":

Nothing before, nothing behind;
The steps of faith
Fall on the seeming void, and find
The Rock beneath.

What if we look to the future, and each step takes us into the "seeming void?" Does not the Bible answer that question for us over and over again? Always, the people of God *have lived by faith*. Abraham left his fatherland for an *unknown* country which God would give him. Later, he prepared to offer on the altar his beloved son, Isaac—even though it made *absolutely no sense*! The future certainly looked *bleak* for young David as he challenged the mighty Goliath. Peter and John faced *prison or even death* if they did not stop preaching the Gospel. Yet, they said, "We cannot help speaking about what we have seen and heard" (Acts 4:20). The Apostle Paul voiced the convictions of all believers through all the generations when he wrote, "If God is for us, who can be against us?" (Rom. 8:31).

☺ Smile Awhile!

Mr Kyle, age two: His mommy heard him yell, "Help! Help! Help!" What could be wrong, thought his mommy as she ran to his aid. When she reached him, he said: "My string got me!" He had pulled a string out of his sock!

Obstacles? Inadequacy? Insecurity? An uncertain future? Those words are a perfect description of believers in the Scriptures; for them the steps of faith were *always* falling on "seeming void." Yet, courage was found; fearful steps landed on the *Rock beneath*. Hebrews 11 gives the perfect formula for finding courage: "By faith . . . By faith . . . By faith. . . ." Paul asserted repeatedly the importance of faith in the believer's life: "For in the gospel a righteousness from God is revealed, a righteousness that is by faith from first to last, just as it is written: 'The righteous will live by faith'" (Romans 1:17).

Mountains & Mustard Seeds

Jesus once asked, "When the Son of Man comes, will he find faith on the earth?" (Luke 18:8). Our Lord said, "... if you have faith as small as a mustard seed, you can say to this mountain, 'Move from here to there' and it will move. Nothing will be impossible for you" (Matt. 17:20). In a devotional moment, I once felt compelled to express Jesus' words in a poem which I entitled, "Of Mountains and Mustard Seeds."

Mountain, mountain, O, so tall.
Mustard seed, mustard seed, O, so small.
Mountain, mountain: immovable, invincible—
incredibly strong!
Mustard seed, mustard seed: little, insignificant—not
wide or long!
YET!
YET!
Mountain, mountain: giant boulders, trees that reach
the sky.
Mustard seed, mustard seed: tiny, delicate, scarcely
seen by the human eye.
YET!
YET!

This doesn't make sense; it's so absurd;
But the words were spoken by Jesus and they must
be heard:
"...if you have faith as small as a mustard seed, you
can say to this mountain, 'Move from here to there'
and it will move."

Look out monstrous mountain;
here comes the mighty mustard seed!

The Everlasting God

What is the antidote for the tigers that stalk us day and night? It is courage born of faith in a God who never leaves us. Trusting Him, take your tiger by the ears and shake him until his teeth rattle! Isaiah says it best:

> Do you not know? Have you not heard? The Lord is the everlasting God, the Creator of the ends of the earth. He will not grow tired or weary, and his understanding no one can fathom. He gives strength to the weary and increases the power of the weak. [30] Even youths grow tired and weary, and young men stumble and fall; [31] but those who hope in the Lord will renew their strength. They will soar on wings like eagles; they will run and not grow weary (Isaiah 40:28-31).

Chapter Eleven

Anger and Adoration

Celebration or Agitation?

Shall I live a life of celebration and joy, or shall I live a life of agitation, irritation, and unhappiness? For me, the choice is between *anger* or *adoration*. Anger is sometimes explosive, *rage incarnated*. At a family meal when I was a boy, my father, in a verbal fight with my mother, grabbed a bowl of beans and slammed it against the wall; that's rage! But anger can take different, less obvious forms, as in the person who just complains about everything. Consider the person who is hyper-critical and finds fault with everyone. I had a man in one of the congregations I served who came in every Monday and griped about the church service the day before. It didn't matter if the attendance was up and people were being converted, he found something wrong! People who have these types of oppositional personalities would deny that they are angry, but that is often the case. Also, impatience can be a form of repressed anger. Notice that unhealthy anger is *me-centered.* Adoration, on the other hand, is *God-centered*. In a previous chapter I indicated that the more time I spend thinking about myself, the more miserable I find myself. Conversely, the more I focus on God and on others, the more peaceful I become.

Consider these contrasts between anger and adoration:

Sinful Anger is Me-Centered.
Soulful Adoration is God-Centered.

Anger says I matter most.
Adoration says God matters most.

Anger gives birth to aggravation, agitation, impatience, resentment.
Adoration gives birth to praise, gratitude, joy, patience, contentment.

Anger grows in the soil of pride—even arrogance.
Adoration grows in the soil of humility—self-sacrifice.

<u>About Anger</u>

Let's think first about *anger*. To be angry implies displeasure, indignation, and feelings of personal injustice or injury. Of itself, anger is not wrong. Indeed, in Scripture God sometimes became angry. Paul instructs the Ephesians: "'In your anger do not sin': Do not let the sun go down while you are still angry, [27] and do not give the devil a foothold" (Eph. 4:26-27). At what point does anger become sinful? Anger is sinful when it rises too soon and without reflection. Also, when it is disproportionate to the offense, or taken out on an innocent party. And, of course, anger is wrong when it leads one to seek revenge (Matt. 5:22; Eph. 4:26; Col. 3:8).

Have you noticed how our culture seems saturated with angry, agitated people? Consider "road rage" as an example. Hardly a week goes by that a serious accident does not occur because of "road rage"; in some instances, people die in these encounters! Sometimes, one enraged person will pull out a gun and shoot into an offending vehicle. Many people live with a "hair trigger"; it takes little to wound their pride and cause them to explode. Woe be to the man or woman who is in their path! A recent article from the paper told of an incident in an upscale retirement home. One man was picking through the lettuce at a salad bar, and a couple of others were offended. Soon a fight broke out and the police had to be called. Some of these folks were in their seventies and eighties! My response: "They are too soon old, and too late smart!" Will Rogers used to say, "People who fly into a rage always make a bad landing."

My brother is a policeman in Indianapolis, and I have spent time with him while he's on duty. One night a man shot and killed his brother in a fight over *the last cupcake*! Can you imagine spending life in jail over a crime like that? I am reminded of Paul's description of the "sinful nature" in Galatians: "The acts of the sinful nature are obvious: sexual immorality, impurity and debauchery; [20] idolatry and witchcraft; hatred, discord, jealousy, fits of rage, selfish ambition, dissensions, factions [21] and envy; drunkenness, orgies, and the like. I warn you, as I did before, that those who live like this will not inherit the kingdom of God" (Gal. 5:19-21).

One day I was pulling into a bank parking lot to cash a check. As I did so, another man was driving out of the parking lot in my direction; but he was in the entrance lane. The exit was on the other side of the bank, and there wasn't room for both of us. I could not back up because of traffic on the busy road behind me. I thought nothing of this young man's mistake; I had done the same thing before learning the proper entrance and exit. His mistake could be easily corrected; all he had to do was back up and turn around. But suddenly he blared his horn, jumped out of his car, and began shouting obscenities. I thought, "He must be mad at someone else; he could not possibly be angry at me for simply driving into the parking lot." The next thing I knew, the fellow was standing at my window insisting that I get out of my car and fight. His face was red; obviously he overflowed with rage. If he had possessed a gun, I think he would have shot me. Imagine the headline in the paper: "Local minister arrested for fighting in bank parking lot!" In spite of the busy road behind me, I backed out and drove off. As I did so, I said to myself, "What was that all about?"

I wish I could say that the kinds of angry dispositions I am describing only exist "out there"—in the world, that is. But, in point of fact, I hear often of episodes of anger and rage *in churches!* I speak of people who worship in the same building, but despise each other—even refuse to speak! How can we possibly hope to experience the "peace that transcends understanding" if we are seething cauldrons of spite and irritation? In his Philippian letter, Paul addressed two ladies by name: "I plead with Euodia and I plead with Syntyche to agree with each other in the Lord" (Philip. 4:2). The operative words in this verse are "agree" and "in the Lord." I am not suggesting that believers must see every issue in the same way. To have differing opinions is natural; but to love and accept people who take opposite perspectives *is Christian*! Hence the saying, "To err is human; to forgive, divine." Churches fuss and divide over issues like *music styles*. Believe me, I have my preferences in music, but I am not about to quit the church if the majority of the worshipers disagree with me. That doesn't mean, of course, that I might not turn off my hearing aid. But I promise you, I won't take it out and throw it at the worship leader!

☺ Smile Awhile!

Mr Kyle, age three: He was getting ready to go to the park with his mommy when he started throwing a fit. His mommy said, "Go ahead and have your fit, and then we'll go." While continuing his kicking, Kyle cried, "I wanna' have my fit!"

Do you know people who just seem to be agitated about something all the time? “Hey, Fred, I hope you are having a good day!” *Fred:* “Well, I’ll have you know that I am not having a good day, and it’s none of your business!” I’m reminded of the fellow of whom it was said, “He’s the most even tempered person I know; he’s mad all the time!” Paul pleaded with the Philippians to be united, to get along with each other: “. . . then make my joy complete by being like-minded, having the same love, being one in spirit and purpose. [3] Do nothing out of selfish ambition or vain conceit, but in humility consider others better than yourselves. [4] Each of you should look not only to your own interests, but also to the interests of others” (Philip. 2:2-4). Paul puts his finger on the heart of the problem: “selfish ambition,” “vain conceit,” and a lack of “humility.” One of the most important, yet difficult things to do is to “consider others better than yourselves.” That is, we must get rid of that subtle, but deadly sense of superiority that causes us to inwardly assume: “*God has made me a bit superior to others. If they would just listen to me, they could get their lives together!*” In one sense, sinful anger is a form of self-worship—making one’s self God! My poem reflects the perspective of the self-centered who await their coronation, *for surely they should be crowned king (or queen!).*

"I Will Raise My Throne!"

I'm a star; you are a stone!
I'm a dog; you are a bone!
I'm a lion; you are a mouse!
I'm a spider; you are a louse!
I'm a king; you are a slave!
I'm a general; you are a private!
I'm a horse; you are a mule!
I am wise; you are a fool!
I am smart; you are dumb!
I am rich; you are a bum!
"I Will Raise My Throne!"

☺ **Smile Awhile!**

From Miss Adrian at age six: Her little sister, Allison, had a *wart* on her foot, which was getting her a lot of attention *and colorful band-aids*. Said Adrian: "I wish I had a wart!"

Adoration: Yearning For God

Adoration, as mentioned above, is God-centered. It is the highest form of worship. When we praise God and thank him for his love and care, that is adoration. Writes Richard Foster: "Adoration is the spontaneous yearning of the heart to worship, honor, magnify, and bless God." The Psalms overflow with adoration. Consider these verses from Psalm 96:1-3:

"Sing to the Lord a new song;
sing to the Lord, all the earth.
[2] Sing to the Lord, praise his name;
proclaim his salvation day after day.
[3] Declare his glory among the nations,
his marvelous deeds among all peoples."

Or consider Isaiah's rapturous experience of the Almighty in the temple as recorded in Isaiah 6. Unusual creatures called "Seraphs" surround the throne of God and cry out to God:

"Holy, holy, holy is the Lord Almighty;
the whole earth is full of his glory"
(Isaiah 6:3).

The Apostle Paul instructed believers to *live* in a spirit of *gratitude, worship, and praise*. We are to cultivate a sense of God's presence: "the Lord is near" (Phil. 4:5); and to "pray continually" (I Thess. 5:17). As alcohol controls the lives of some individuals, we are to become *inebriated* with God's Spirit. That is, we are to allow God's Spirit to take control of our thoughts and actions. Hear the Apostle Paul:

> Do not get drunk on wine, which leads to debauchery. Instead, be filled with the Spirit. [19] Speak to one another with psalms, hymns, and spiritual songs. Sing and make music in your heart to the Lord, [20] always giving thanks to God the Father for everything, in the name of our Lord Jesus Christ (Eph. 5:18-20).

When we begin living to praise and adore God, anger—in whatever form—loses its grip on us. The joy of the Lord and the wonder of grace capture our hearts; *celebration* and *doxology* then describe our natural predisposition. Remember when Paul and Silas were in a prison cell at Philippi? What were they doing? "About midnight Paul and Silas were praying and singing hymns to God, and the other prisoners were listening to them" (Acts 16:25). Singing at midnight? I have trouble even staying awake until that hour, let alone singing and praying! I knew a Christian man who carried a hymnal with him wherever he went; any appropriate time he would sing hymns of praise to God. So then, which house do we live in? The house that *anger* builds, or the house that *adoration* builds? I remind the reader of the question that is central to the purpose of this book: *Does your commitment to Christ make a difference in your internal world?*

Prayer: Filled With His Presence

"Father, to be filled with your presence is to be ever-filled with joy. It's like an underground spring that never runs dry—even in a season of drought. Springs of living water bubble up from inside. Living Water quenches the thirst of my innermost soul. Thank you, Father. AMEN."

Chapter Twelve

Life and Death

KNOCK, KNOCK!

"Yes, who's there?"

"It's me, Death."

"Well, what in the world do you want?"

"I want you. I have come for you!"

"There must be a mistake. I'm young, healthy; my whole life is ahead of me!"

"I make no mistakes. Let's go!"

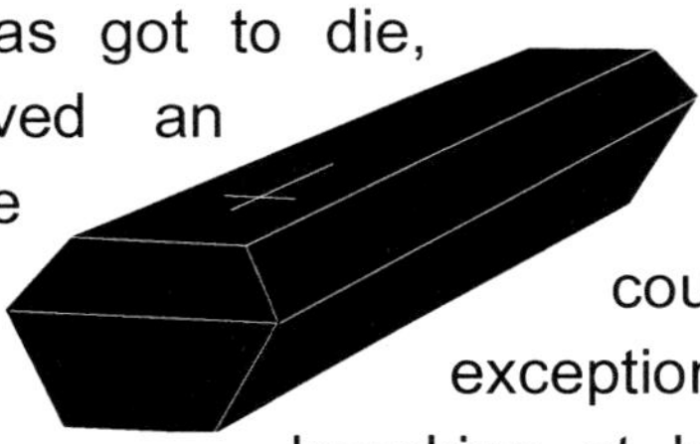

William Saroyan's statement, made five days before his death, has become somewhat famous: "Everybody has got to die, but I have always believed an exception would be made in my case." Of course, there are no exceptions; death will come knocking at both your door and mine. He doesn't even bother to set up an appointment; most of the time he just barges in when we least expect him. We don't know when or how, but we all recognize that each day the probability for that knock increases. In his epistle, James writes, "What is your life? You are a mist that appears for a little while and then vanishes" (James 4:14). For unbelievers, death is a long, cold walk into eternal nothingness. For believers, however, death is the gateway to a new and better life. In Scripture, death is never treated as a friend; in it the Evil One wins a *partial* and *limited* victory. “Limited” because *it appears* that evil and death have won the final battle. But be not deceived by *appearances*! Arguing from the resurrection of Jesus, Paul asserts: "Death has been swallowed up in victory” (1 Cor. 15:54). God raised his Son from the dead! Christians should view their death differently than those who see the grave as eternal nothingness. Certainly, Paul believed that to be the case: “Brothers, we do not want you to be ignorant about those who fall asleep, or to grieve like the rest of men, who have no hope” (1 Thess. 4:13). Through his resurrection, Jesus removed the “sting of death” (1 Cor. 15:55). Paul wrote, “For the trumpet will sound, the dead will be raised imperishable, and we will be changed” (1Cor. 15:52). I think it would be accurate to say that the Grim Reaper knocked on Paul's door, and Paul invited him in for tea and biscuits! Listen to the Apostle’s triumphant proclamation from Second Corinthians:

Behold...
The Lord

> Therefore we are always confident and know that as long as we are at home in the body we are away from the Lord. We live by faith, not by sight. We are confident, I say, and

> would prefer to be away from the body and at home with the Lord. So we make it our goal to please him, whether we are at home in the body or away from it (II Cor. 5:6-9).

☺ **Smile Awhile!**

From Miss Allison, age six: In Allison's family, a great aunt and a great grandparent had died within a couple of months of each other. Also, they had lost their dog whose name was Blackberry. Allison was praying for their meal when she added these sentences: "Lord, please help us. There aren't many of us left down here!"

Fearing Death

Am I saying that Christians will have *no fear of death*? Not necessarily. Certainly believers will fear death *less* than those who have no hope of eternal life; but the fear of death is a universal human experience. Perhaps Christians don't fear *death* as much as they fear *dying*; at least that is true for me. We can't help but wonder: "When and how will I die?" Will it be a sudden heart attack in the middle of the night or a long, protracted illness that robs me of my personality? I don't fear my own death, as much as I fear losing the ones I love. My wife and I have always said that we would like to live until we are eighty-five and then die together on the same night! Of course, almost certainly, that won't happen.

Do you remember when the *inevitability* of death became a reality for you? For me it happened with the death of my father, which I mentioned in an earlier chapter. We had talked about going on a long fishing trip to Canada. At last, the plans were made; we were going to leave on a Thursday night, after I finished classes at Lincoln Christian Seminary. My wife greeted me with a sad countenance, and asked me to be seated. As gently as possible, she gave me the news: "David, your father had a massive heart attack this afternoon, and died immediately." I was shocked. My father was only forty-six; he had no history of serious heart problems. Before his death, I believed that death happened *to other people*. Now I realized that death would happen to *mine—to me*! All of us know that, at any moment, the Grim Reaper might step out of the shadow and lay his hand on our shoulder: "Its your turn!" Being human means living with death's reality. However, *being Christian means living with death's hope.* From a Christian perspective, the worst thing that happens to you (your death), becomes *the best thing that can happen to you*. In death, we walk the dark valley; but just on the other side dawns a new day which is bathed in brilliant Son-light. Death conveys us into a life that has no shadow: "The city does not need the sun or the moon to shine on it, for the glory of God gives it light, and the Lamb is its lamp" (Rev. 21:23). I like the way Ken Gire says it: "The soul is

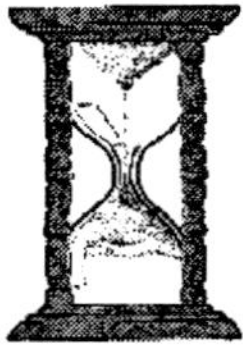

extraterrestrial, fitted for heaven. It breathes other air, eats other food, [drinks other water] . . . ." Hear the confidence of Joseph Addison:

The Soul

The Soul, secure in her existence, smiles
At drawn dagger, and defies its point:
The stars shall fade away, the sun himself
Grow dim with age, and nature sink in years:
But thou shalt flourish in immortal youth,
Unhurt amidst the war of elements,
The wrecks of matter, the crash of worlds!
(From Cato)

Of all the people who have attended our services at Summit Tower Apartments, Cleo was one of the sweetest. She was in her eighties when we first met her. Cleo suffered from extreme osteoporosis; her body was literally bent at a right angle. When she walked, with the aid of a walker, she had no choice but to stare at the ground. Though extremely frail of body, Cleo's mind was in good working order until the last few months of her life. She loved beautiful, bright clothing, and would match gorgeous earrings to her outfit. Cleo was also a poet, and I read some of her poems in my sermons. It took her a long time to dress for church services, yet, she seldom missed. One Sunday she whispered something to Mary Faith, which brought a chuckle to them both. Afterwards, I asked Mary Faith, "What did Cleo say that was so funny?" Cleo had said, "I barely made it to church. I couldn't get my bra on, but at least I'm here!"

When I preached Cleo's funeral, I felt sad; but I knew her time had arrived. Her body could no longer sustain an enjoyable quality of life. I believe she's now singing praises to the God she faithfully served and loved. And if I know Cleo, she probably has the brightest robes of any saint in heaven—with large, colorful earrings to match! At Cleo's funeral, I tried to honor her God, and also pay tribute to this spirited Christian lady. I wrote a piece of verse in her memory which I entitled, "Free!" Because it asserts the Christian's hope, I use it to close this volume.

FREE!

And thus we find ourselves in a prison cell called "time"—
confined behind bars called "space."
But someday our Father will say:
"My child, come out!
You do not need to live any longer in those tight quarters!
Step out from that prison cell!
Now, isn't that much better?
What's that upon your arm? A watch?
Throw it away!
You need not a timepiece in this new heaven and earth—this is Eternity!

Now, go as far as you wish in any direction!
Fly like a bird; explore the galaxies!
It's all yours, because it's all mine.
My child, I have set you free from 'time' and 'space'!
Free! You are free from death itself!
By my grace, you are free!!"

"And they will reign for ever and forever"

(Rev. 22:5)

Prayer: "To Him Who Is Able ..."

"To him who is able to keep you from falling and to present you before his glorious presence without fault and with great joy—[25] to the only God our Savior be glory, majesty, power, and authority, through Jesus Christ our Lord, before all ages, now and forevermore! Amen" (Jude 1:24-25).

Sources Cited

Eller, Vernard. *The Simple Life: The Christian Stance Toward Possessions.* Grand Rapids, Michigan: Eerdmans Publishing Company, 1973.

Frankl, Viktor E. *Man's Search for Meaning.* New York: Simon & Schuster, Inc., 1984.

Gire, *Ken. Windows of the Soul: Experiencing God in New Ways*. Grand Rapids, Michigan: Zondervan Publishing House, 1996.

Karon, Jan. *Out to Canaan* (The Mitford Series). New York: Penguin Books, 1997.

Miller, Calvin. *The Unchained Soul.* Minneapolis, Minnesota: Bethany House Publishers, 1995.

Miller, Calvin. *The Table of Inwardness*. Downers Grove, Illinois: Inter-Varsity Press, 1984.

Nouwen, Henri M. *The Way of the Heart*. New York: Seabury Press, 1981.

Poems for Life: Quotable Verse from Seers and Singers of Yesterday and Today. Compiled by Thomas Curtis Clark. New York: Willett, Clark & Company, 1941.

Rhodes, Tricia McCary. *The Soul at Rest*. Minneapolis: Bethany House Publishers, 1996.

Van De Weyer, Robert (compiler). *The Harper Collins Book of Prayers: A Treasury of Prayer Through the Ages*. Edison, New Jersey: Castle Books, 1997.